D0435119

THE LONG TAKE

THE LONG TAKE

or

A Way to Lose More Slowly

Robin Robertson

PICADOR

First published 2018 by Picador
an imprint of Pan Macmillan
20 New Wharf Road, London N1 9RR
Associated companies throughout the world
www.panmacmillan.com

ISBN 978-1-5098-4688-7

5 7 9 8 6

A CIP catalogue record for this book is available from the British Library.

Printed and bound by CPI Group (UK) Ltd, Croydon, CR0 4YY

Visit **www.picador.com** to read more about all our books
and to buy them. You will also find features, author interviews and
news of any author events, and you can sign up for e-newsletters
so that you're always first to hear about our new releases.

cos cheum nach gabh tilleadh

CONTENTS

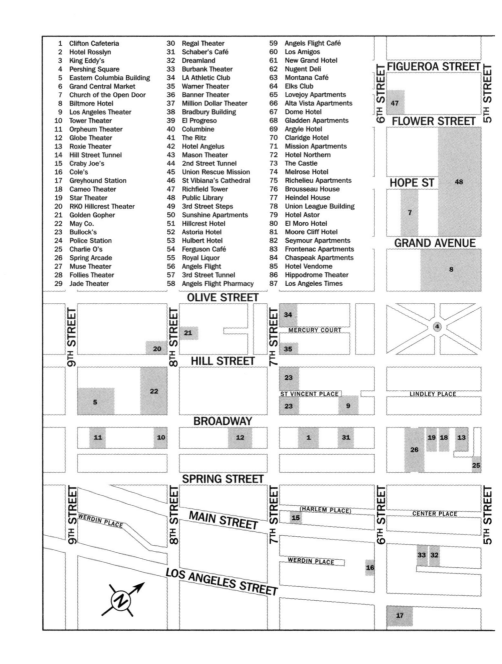

1 Clifton Cafeteria	30 Regal Theater	59 Angels Flight Café
2 Hotel Rosslyn	31 Schaber's Café	60 Los Amigos
3 King Eddy's	32 Dreamland	61 New Grand Hotel
4 Pershing Square	33 Burbank Theater	62 Nugent Deli
5 Eastern Columbia Building	34 LA Athletic Club	63 Montana Café
6 Grand Central Market	35 Warner Theater	64 Elks Club
7 Church of the Open Door	36 Banner Theater	65 Lovejoy Apartments
8 Biltmore Hotel	37 Million Dollar Theater	66 Alta Vista Apartments
9 Los Angeles Theater	38 Bradbury Building	67 Dome Hotel
10 Tower Theater	39 El Progreso	68 Gladden Apartments
11 Orpheum Theater	40 Columbine	69 Argyle Hotel
12 Globe Theater	41 The Ritz	70 Claridge Hotel
13 Roxie Theater	42 Hotel Angelus	71 Mission Apartments
14 Hill Street Tunnel	43 Mason Theater	72 Hotel Northern
15 Craby Joe's	44 2nd Street Tunnel	73 The Castle
16 Cole's	45 Union Rescue Mission	74 Melrose Hotel
17 Greyhound Station	46 St Vibiana's Cathedral	75 Richelieu Apartments
18 Cameo Theater	47 Richfield Tower	76 Brousseau House
19 Star Theater	48 Public Library	77 Heindel House
20 RKO Hillcrest Theater	49 3rd Street Steps	78 Union League Building
21 Golden Gopher	50 Sunshine Apartments	79 Hotel Astor
22 May Co.	51 Hillcrest Hotel	80 El Moro Hotel
23 Bullock's	52 Astoria Hotel	81 Moore Cliff Hotel
24 Police Station	53 Hulbert Hotel	82 Seymour Apartments
25 Charlie O's	54 Ferguson Café	83 Frontenac Apartments
26 Spring Arcade	55 Royal Liquor	84 Chaspeak Apartments
27 Muse Theater	56 Angels Flight	85 Hotel Vendome
28 Follies Theater	57 3rd Street Tunnel	86 Hippodrome Theater
29 Jade Theater	58 Angels Flight Pharmacy	87 Los Angeles Times

FIGUEROA STREET

6TH STREET

5TH STREET

FLOWER STREET

47

HOPE ST

48

7

GRAND AVENUE

8

OLIVE STREET

9TH STREET

8TH STREET

7TH STREET

34

21

MERCURY COURT

20

35

HILL STREET

23

22

ST VINCENT PLACE

LINDLEY PLACE

5

23

9

BROADWAY

11

10

12

1

31

19 18 13

26

25

SPRING STREET

9TH STREET

8TH STREET

7TH STREET

6TH STREET

5TH STREET

WERDIN PLACE

MAIN STREET

(HARLEM PLACE)

15

CENTER PLACE

WERDIN PLACE

33 32

16

LOS ANGELES STREET

17

N

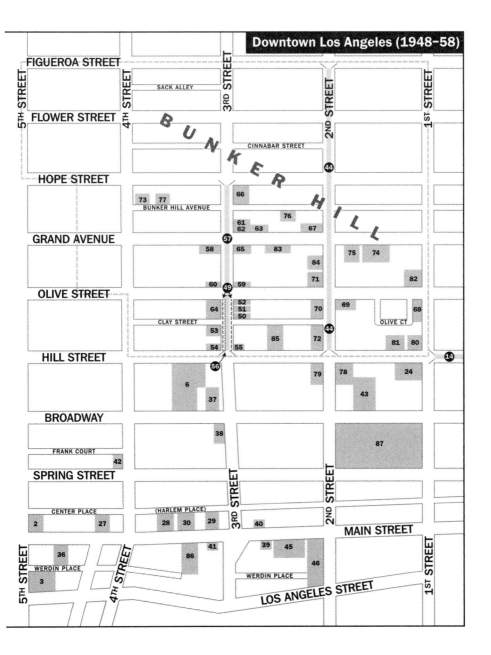

Downtown Los Angeles (1948–58)

FIGUEROA STREET

5TH STREET

4TH STREET

3RD STREET

2ND STREET

1ST STREET

SACK ALLEY

FLOWER STREET

BUNKER HILL

CINNABAR STREET

HOPE STREET

44

73   77
BUNKER HILL AVENUE

66

76

GRAND AVENUE

61
62   63

67

57

58   65   83

75   74

84

60   59

71

82

OLIVE STREET

49

52
51
50

70   69

68

64

CLAY STREET

53

OLIVE CT

HILL STREET

54   55

85   72

81   80

56

14

79   78   24

6

43

37

BROADWAY

38

FRANK COURT

87

42

SPRING STREET

CENTER PLACE

(HARLEM PLACE)

2   27

28   30   29

40

MAIN STREET

3RD STREET

2ND STREET

1ST STREET

41

39   45

86

46

5TH STREET

36

WERDIN PLACE

WERDIN PLACE

3

4TH STREET

LOS ANGELES STREET

THE LONG TAKE

1946

And there it was: the swell
and glitter of it like a standing wave –
the fabled, smoking ruin, the new towers rising
through the blue,
the ranked array of ivory and gold, the glint,
the glamour of buried light
as the world turned round it
very slowly
this autumn morning, all amazed.

And it stayed there, watching,
as they made toward it,
the truck-driver and the young man,
under pylons, wires, utility poles,
past warehouses, container parks,
deserted lots, between the long
oily marshes, landfill sites and swamps,
before slipping down
under the Hudson, and coming up
on the other side
to find a black wetness
of streets trashed and empty
and the city gone.

'Try the docks. They can always use men.'

★

It was in me, burning like a coal-seam fire. The road.

Back there in Broad Cove, on the island, it was just working the mines or the boats. Taking on the habit of the old ones – the long stare out to sea – becoming like a thorn tree, twisted hard to the shape of the wind, its grain following the grain of the weather; cloth caps and tweed, ruddy, raw-boned faces, wet eyes, silences that lasted weeks; the women wringing red hands or dishcloths or the necks of chickens just to make more silence.

★

He walks. That is his name and nature.
Rows of buildings, all alike,
doors and windows, people going in, looking out;
inside – halls and stairs, halls and stairs,
and more doors, opening and closing.
Street after street of buildings, all the same.
People, all the same.

The clutter and color: everything
moving on the street, and across it, straight lines
and diagonals. Drug-stores, grocery stores,
snack joints, diners. Missions. Bars.
Blocks. Corners. Intersections.
A dropped crate or a child's shout, or car
backfiring, and he's in France again,
that taste in his mouth. Coins. Cordite. Blood.

4

So loud. And bright. No place to ease the eyes. To hide. So this is what happens between one night and the next: this is day. A never-ending rehearsal with a cast that changes all the time but never gets it right. Dropping things. Walking into each other. Tripping on the curb. Every door, every window, opening and closing, automobiles sliding past, the calls of the vendors, shrieks of children, horses and carts, trolley-cars and delivery trucks. People in a hurry, in every direction, wired to some kind of a grid. Maybe from up high you could see a plan for it all, like a model-train layout. Not down here though. Everything's going too fast and there are too many people and cars and I'm holding on to this stop-sign because I'm frightened and I know I'm going to die.

A hard migraine of color-clash, daggering light,
and sun laid out everywhere in white flags.
Not a shadow in this world.

★

The road invisible under heavy snow: a clean and softened land, fluent and dazzling down to the ocean's slate. The only color is the lichen clinging to twigs, bright as pollen, and back at the house, the berries of the rowan tree, one arm across the door.

★

Night.

The city's gone.
In its place, this gray stone maze, this
locked geometry of shadows, blind and black,
and angles hurt into the sky, symmetries breaking

5

and snapping back into line.
The green Zs of fire-escapes; wires criss-
crossing what's left of the light
to a tight mesh.
The buildings close
around a dead-end, then
spring open to the new future: repetition,
back-tracking, error, loss.

★

*Father just stood at the door. 'The war was one thing, but this is another. You're
the first of us to leave in a hundred and seventy years.'*

★

He wanted to see this country, so he did:
the benches of Hanover Square at dawn,
Fanelli's, the Spot, the White Horse,
the parks, the pawn shops, the 15-cent diners,
the Green Door, the Marathon, the Garden Bar,
a Beekman Street archway with a drink after dark.

He'd surprise his reflection in a store window:
see the curly-haired boy with his fishing pole;
the skinny white soldier with blank eyes,
getting thinner.

He walks among ghosts.
Never sees the same face twice.
He navigated by the sun

when he could find it between the buildings, the canyons.
The subways are rivers, underground,
flash-flooding every five minutes
in a pulse of people.
People from all over, all colors, a hundred languages:
Italian, Polish, Russian, German, Yiddish,
Spanish from the Mexicans, the Puerto Ricans,
that *Chinese* – like a tape running backward, at speed.

People; just like him.
Having given up the country for the city,
boredom for fear, the faces
gather here in these streets
like spectators in a dream.
They wanted to be anonymous
not swallowed whole, not to disappear.
Now they spend their days on South Street
or down at the Battery, their nights
in the Bowery flophouses, the cage-hotels,
tight packed like herrings in a creel.

★

Cold as Candlemas. A skin of ice
on the water-glass by the bed
is the only thing that doesn't shake under the rails
of the 3rd Avenue El overhead.
Through the gray net curtain,
above the tenements outside, the sky
jitters awake like a loose connection;
lightning glows behind the walls of cloud.

Somewhere, up north of here,
is the Chrysler, and the Empire State.
Somewhere south there's Liberty.

★

Going down into the subway by the same metaled stairs
as that troop ship in Southampton: the hot churn
and thundering of the machine,
riveted corridors and halls, darkness, sudden light, dead air,
the clattering echo of footsteps on steel.
The white, unseeing eyes.

★

*It was all about timing. Waiting to jump from the scramble net down the side of
the merchant ship to the LCA below. Trying to find the rhythm of it: the swell
of the water, the boats colliding. Your best chance was just before the landing craft
slammed against the ship's hull. Mistiming the jump meant drowning or crushing.
You got it right. Picked yourself up. The steel deck slippery with vomit.*

★

Up on the El, trying to keep warm
near the old pot-bellied stove
by the change-booth and turnstiles,
he liked to lean over,
watch the people seething below:
a river of hats
following a current, streaming round obstacles
then re-forming: gray and brown and black.

8

It came to him then.
You can never step into the same city twice.
That was it.
Living here was like trying to cross a river in spate
and he'd just found his footing,
or at least a way of looking at it – from a distance.
Close up, nothing here was beautiful,
and so much now was a close-up shot.
He needed to re-calibrate, focus on all this
new geometry, light and shadow, black and white:
take the long view. Like staring out to sea.

★

Sea-sick from the gridded streets,
the brick towers and mirrors and
black-drop canyons
he fixed, queasily,
on the steady line of Brooklyn Bridge.
He found a room, a fifth-floor walk-up on Water Street
for six dollars a week, and no down-payment needed
for the de-mobbed
with his veteran pin.
He got hired the next day in the shape-up;
found himself a box-hook and a job on the docks.

Ice webbed the wooden pilings,
the ice-spill opaque and raised
and slippery-smooth like dried glue.
Back home, the sea would be chipped granite,
shale, anthracite blue; terns sipping the waves,

cheeping low over a run of mackerel
before the whelming breach of a humpback, or a pilot whale.

★

The smell of stewed tea and wet clothes, smuts from the oil lamps, the valves
in the radio like embers, glowing; the penetrating, never-ending rain — and
winter, like a white door closing for six months. Skipping Mass at St Margaret's.
Gazing out over the gunmetal sea.

★

He would watch the river all day for that moment:
when the tide reaches slack
and the bottles afloat on the surface are completely still.

The slap of waves against the rocky shingle
like the distant crackle and crump
of small arms or mortars, or the flap of wet tarpaulin.

A block away, in the pearl dusk, some whore
worked-over for a dollar bill; dancing now,
face down, in the Hudson.

★

In the bath-house, where he went every week,
the usual hair and yellowed Kleenex in the shower-room's gutter,
the Band-Aids in the pool; the usual chat
in the steam-room, sitting on the slatted wood,
no dog-tags now, just the St Christopher:

'Hey, bud, what goes? Where you staying?'
'The Mills. Flophouse on Bleecker – a real dump,
but it'll do till I get things straightened out.
What about you?'
'Got outta the joint last week. Gonna see a friend of mine.
Make a meet, y'know? Says he's got a job for me.'
'No kidding?
When the whole thing was over,
when we got back home,
I thought there'd be a job for me too.'

★

Then the slow retreat of winter. Spring's advent and reprieve. You'd see drift ice from the Arctic, which sometimes passed so near you could hear the songs of the seals voyaging there on those gray shelves of ice.

★

At night, the river rolls and turns like oil
under the bridges,
in through the slips.
He walked for hours –
following the glow
in the sky uptown he'd been told
was the lights of Times Square –
his shadow moving with him
below the streetlamps: dense, tight,
very black and sharp, foreshortened, but already
starting to lengthen as he goes, attenuating
to a weak stain. Then back in

under another streetlight, shadow
darkening again, clean and hard.
Who he really is, or was,
lies somewhere in between.

★

Watching *Ride the Pink Horse*
then *Out of the Past* the same week at the Majestic:
New Mexico and Acapulco on the screen, with ice and rain outside.
The projector's cone of light above their heads in the darkness,
the way the smoke from their cigarettes
went up into it, twisted and bloomed.

★

*The hawthorn hangs like mist in the valleys. The gorse bright against the melting
snow, with its smell of coconut on the high sea cliffs; the mayflower opening its
sweetness in the black wood.*

★

He moved to the fish market
where the work was easier, safer, the crates smaller,
and you could see those lovelies, from all down the coast:
Portland, Maine, to Cape Canaveral.
Late April, into May, was flounder, whiting, monkfish, hake,
striped bass and mackerel, and, briefly, Hudson River shad.
Shad fillet and roe from Carmine's or Whyte's:
the best fish he'd had in years.

12

One day he lifted some lobster boxes onto his barrow,
and stared at the stamp showing
`MacLeod's Point, Ingonish, N.S.`
He saw the little harbor, the blue boats,
Star of the Sea, The Rover, Màire Bàn;
the old hand-woven pots.
The faces of the very fishermen.

★

*The bay boiling with the capelin scull coming in, and the codfish after them –
and after them the heave of whales. Like waves of black weed the small fish roll
and beach, twining and flipping silver on the sand, where the women wait with
their nets and baskets, on the same stretch of shore where the capelin come, each
year, to spawn, to signal spring.*

★

Central Park: a clearing
in this forest of stone;
a fire-gap among the ziggurats
that's cut in living green.
In the stringency of early-morning light
he walked through a may-storm of petals,
the pink of cherry-blossom thick in the gutter
and filling every crack in the sidewalk.
He heard a sound like a slide whistle:
whoit whoit whoit whoit
and there, in that tree, unbelievably,
a red bird.

★

New York's got just about anything you want. It's like a market: a place where everything's available, everything's for sale. But it's all finite, already disappearing. So we want it now; we have to have it *now*.

A cardinal. One day I'll learn all their names.

May, 47

★

He was standing in an east-side bar, nursing a double,
when the one next to him says:
'You see him in the corner, friend?' pointing with his eyes.
The old guy they're looking at is looking at the bottle
as he pours, the beer going greedy into the glass.
His face a knuckle:
tight red, white where the muscle moved;
putty-colored teeth; eyes countersunk.
'Story is, he used to run with Maranzano.
They say he knocked a guy down once,
put a pen in his ear and kicked it home.
Then the heat came down when they got his boss
and he moved to Jersey, started as a ring-fighter,
had an act where he dressed as a fisherman,
wrestled an octopus.'
The beer is poured.
Dark vertical lines drop from the sides of his mouth
like a ventriloquist's dummy.
As he swallows
the slot moves up and down.
The friend shakes his head. '*Some guy.*'

★

In the summer, under the slats and latticework
of the El, you see a net of sun and shadow
dice everyone like vegetables.
The drunks will wake up later, underneath:
grill-marked, lined by light.

★

The papers say
'Keep dogs and cats inside on the Fourth of July'
but nothing about ex-servicemen.
You can't get tanked enough to block
the fireworks' whine, their
door-burst slam, the rustling
shiver as they fail, fissling away.
So he watches the endless red, white and blue,
remembering he's here in the States
not on Juno Beach or Bény-sur-Mer.
Star-rockets burst to their edges
with the sparse bright gold of autumn trees.
He thinks of all those rockets and their cold, thin wooden stems,
five hundred of them
falling back toward him through the night.

★

*All there was in Broad Cove was the ceilidh in the church hall, once a month.
Every family came. The men fingering their collars, the women patting at their
hair. The whiskey and the music loosened both and, soon enough, the children –
wide-eyed at the sight of this transfiguration – were led away by the very old.
We would twist back to catch the last sight of the grown-ups, laughing.*

Their faces in the hall grew redder, eyes brighter, as the strathspeys, slow like waltzes, gave way to hornpipes, jigs – the dances all more furious, till the last reel, and the accordion and fiddle were finally put down.

We'd stand outside in the shadows and wait. There was singing, more laughter, broken glass. Then the fights – the fat, concussive slaps of men on men and the squeals of women – and later, farther off, in under the sugar maples, the loving, which sounded much the same.

★

That time in London, on leave, with a bunch of guys from C Company. 3rd Division had been together for a couple years, training all over. Battle drill in the barracks, landing drill around the coast, and up in Rothesay and Fort William we got both. We were primed by the end, especially us: the North Nova Scotia Highlanders. Ready to go.

We'd aimed for Piccadilly, of course, but the lights were all off and there was no statue: just a big green cone-shaped hoarding, advertising Saving Stamps. We wanted to go dancing, but not with those chippies on the street. Not that kind of dancing. We went through a door under a dead neon sign for Gordon's Gin and got safe underground in a place called Ward's: Ward's Irish House, for Guinness and oysters at the long zinc counter. They had some old boys in a corner with fiddles and a bodhrán and it was all like home again, with the jigs and reels and slow airs. We were told about a good dancehall in Hammersmith, so we struggled up the stairs, and took ourselves west.

One of the boys said Monty had his HQ in some school round here, but we only cared about the Palais and the girls, and it was humming inside, that Saturday night, with the band playing swing tunes nice and loud – Miller, Goodman, Louis Jordan – and the girls so pretty and new.

I said I'd walk her home, but she took me down to the river, right under Hammer-smith Bridge, along the embankment – just the light of the moon on the water. That's all.

That's all I remember.

★

Washing lines
strung between tenements:
the pennants of a black-and-white parade.

★

I think of her all the time, back on the island. Wonder what she's doing. Keep a piece of oak that I carved at work, worked into a heart. Maybe I'll send it to her.

Manhattan's the place for re-invention, mobility, anonymity, where everything is possible. It's what I came for. Every city street is a stage – every stage, a staging of desire.

July, 47

★

Manhattan's twin, her strange, beguiling sister, Coney,
best visited at night, rising up from the sea
ablaze, calling men and women down
toward their dreams and terrors, the white fire
of electricity and light, the chance – in the plummet
of the roller-coaster, the dark-ride, the Wonder Wheel –
for them to hold each other, quickly, somewhere out of sight.

17

Looka! Looka! Looka! Get your tickets here!
Don't hold back, boys and girls! The ride of your life!

Evenings still hot, but a breeze off the sea
and the smell of French fries, candy, girls' perfume.
The lights are so beautiful, and he picks out a rhythm
in the screams and laughter, the rumble
of the rides, the metal's screeling, through the hundred
different fairground tunes, the thousand calls and shouts,
the noise of America at play
with the crush of the Atlantic
breaking under the boardwalk,
steady and slow.
To be young, and *in this world*. Alive!

What'ya waiting for? C'mon, take a ride!
Only a nickel! You'll all come out with a smile!

By day, you can see she's made of pasteboard, held together
by nuts and bolts, metal frames – that the huge clown's head
is chipped, the painted façades all faded, peeling.
Manhattan's the same, just better made.

Looka! Looka! Looka! Watch the pretty lights!
See the funny mirrors! Watch the world twist
and bend and slide out of shape!

Alive! – World's Strangest Freaks – the Smallest Grown Ups
on Earth, Tom Thumb and his Brother, Marian the Headless Girl
from London, Milo the Mule Face Boy, Zip & Pip –
Two Georgia Peaches – the Living Spider Boy,
the Human Ostrich, the Half Man Half Woman – Alive!

Step right up, ladies and gentlemen! Grab a star by the tail!
Take a trip to the moon! Looka! Looka! Looka!

★

The river sweats in its dream.
The balloon on a stick he'd bought from the blind man
has worked its way up to the ceiling.

★

We walked down the choir of the forest carrying the dried-up stalks and pods
of bluebells — our summer rattles — on through the opened trees: our ceremonies of
light in the green cathedrals.

★

These moons in their hundreds, pinked underneath by the beginnings of daylight,
are barrage balloons towed by the boats. Seven thousand in this dawn armada.
Ships and the wakes of ships. As if a giant was drawing them on strings, out from
the harbor. The Channel so thick with traffic you could cross it on the backs of
boats.

★

He'd sleep out on the roof, these nights,
and stare at this city
that's too big to measure,
has too many windows to watch.
And nobody sees or cares anyway,
so nothing matters.

There's no more room in this high city:
all human scale is lost.

★

He dreamt of a giant staircase made of sleeping-platforms, each covered in heavy bedding, each holding people too large for the space. Their feet hang in the faces of those below; their blankets spill down; there is rancor, disagreement. Then it all pulls away and we see the stair is open, without banisters, and is hundreds of feet high, going up – and down – as far as the eye can see.

★

He had to get out of this heat:
away from the stink of Fulton Market.
Get uptown at night, on the El – the fast
slatted bridge over moving light and noise,
poles and wires, poles and wires,
people, cars, all swimming underneath –
to the Street, West 52nd:
Jimmy Ryan's, the Famous Door,
the Three Deuces, the Spotlight, the Downbeat.
This music he'd never heard: that
hit him like a two-by-four –
Lester Young, Powell and Tatum, Dizzy
and Bird, and his favorites,
Johnny Hodges, Ben Webster, and,
best of all, the Hawk.

★

At night the shadows slant and sharpen. By morning, the city has climbed higher still on its gold ledges of light.

September, 47

★

'Up there . . .' he gestured at the bright
jewelry of the towers,
the wasted light of penthouses and suites,
'. . . are all the girls and all the money.
We're down where we belong: chasing deals,
eating shadows.'

'Times Square. Man, that's the place!
Restaurants, clubs, women, cheap liquor. All-night fun.'

★

He remembered every bar as a battlefield
sodden with carnage,
and the blurred ghosts of drinkers,
their glasses emptying, filling, emptying;
the dirt in each corner, dreams and despair.
Winos, lined along the Roxy Grill:
their faces mottled red and white,
congested, misshapen, like someone had
set each head on fire
and put it out with a baseball bat.
People tried to straighten up at Bickford's
where the food's good and cheap
but the last time he went he watched a junky

21

pin a busboy to the table with a fork.
And the women? Try the Pokerino Palace after hours.
He was walking by two weeks ago and this doll emerged,
face sagging like a fallen hem,
asked if he wanted a hit
off her bottle, or maybe a blow–job –
gazed long at the sidewalk, opened wide
then threw out a gray wing of vomit.

*

'Went up the Empire State!
At the top they got this thing, this *observation deck*.
Buddy, you oughtta look at them down there:
milling around, going nowhere,
nowhere to go, no one telling them.'
He stared harder, into the distance.
'Ants don't sleep, you know, they just keep moving.'

*

The falcons hunt from their high palisades, stooping on pigeons: a swift
gray puff-burst.

Down at the bottom, it's just dust-devils, butts and bottle-tops spinning
round and round.

Is this place a giant turbine, endlessly turning, or just a pointless revving
at the lights?

October, 47

*

'Whiskey.'

'Y'wan' a bourbon? It's on special deal.'

'Nah – too sweet. Gimme a rye. Double.'

'Where ya from anyhow?'

'Cape Breton.'

'Huh?'

'It's in Canada.'

'You drink rye in Canada?'

'Yep. Goes good with the seal-liver and the blubber.'

★

In the church hall, slow-dancing with Annie at the Harvest Ball, my dishonor stiff between us like a sword. The stars, when we walked outside. The cool of her hand in mine. Those clean blue eyes.

★

The fear of corridors, elevators, attics, cellars,
windows, doors. Staircases, most of all.
Wading through shadows, black pools,
then a long wedge of light
swinging open at an angle like a curtain
slashed by a knife. The floor tips
and drops away, and the door closes. Ink dark.
White rods slide out of the wall, razor-edged
by shadow, beginning to splay
and take in everything, then
snapping shut. Light locked
in a dark room. This whole city is a trap.

★

'You one of them Reds? One of them infil-traitors?
Sitting there with your book, listening in.'
Walker looked up from his seat in the corner.
'Yeah. I'm talking to you, Mac. You a Commie?'
'Hey, give the guy a break. He's a regular.'
'What's he reading, anyway? Look – I told ya!
Red Harvest, it's called! That proves it.'
'Leave it, Joe. He's not bothering anyone.'
'Joe?' Walker smiled. 'Joe *Stalin?*'
He caught the swinging fist and pushed it down
onto the table, onto his empty shot-glass –
watching the table fill, and Uncle Joe turn gray.

★

*It was dusk. We watched the starlings mass and whirl, then drain from the sky
into a single tree. Then she said my name: that living jolt at the strike when you
feel the fish, switching away.*

Let the sun heat her rock on the island, and let her find a better man than me.

★

*The New Dock, Southampton: vessels moored to the jetty, tied to each other, seven
or eight deep, stretching three miles back. You had to clamber over them to get to
your own. Then guided in convoy through the minefields by green colored lights.
The only sound the engines turning. I'd never seen anything as beautiful as this.
The whole sea black with ships.*

★

In the last splinter of sunlight allowed between the skyscrapers
an old lady is sitting with a book,
moving her chair every quarter of an hour
a little farther down the alleyway.

★

He saw the end of a bar-fight
emptying into the street.
The first plunge jarred on bone
but the second went clean through,
home to the hilt.
Red mists the wall.
The knife is a twisting fish, a bright
torrent, a key
to lift his whole side
up: open him
like a present
laid out in a sheet of blood.

★

'You fight in the war, buddy?'
'. . . Er . . . Yes. Yes, I fought.'
'To save the free world, was it, pal?'
'Something like that.'
'The free world thank you?'
'The French and the Dutch did, eh.'
'Not us, though? Americans?'
'Can't say I've noticed.'
'But then, you're a Canuck.'

★

Sitting high above the sweep of Broad Cove, watching the sun set over Prince Edward Island, the last light catching the end of the yarrow, the leaves of the loosestrife turning red, and the seals asleep on Margaree Island, the Sea Wolf Island, north of here.

Always closer to the exit than the altar, or so my mother said. And now I have cast myself out: into the wilderness, into this city and its rapids. What enormous energy it takes, to fling yourself out of the nest.

★

The trees by the East River have things
snagged in their lowest branches: clothes,
fish-crates, ropes and sacks, bodies sometimes,
people say, trapped there by the tides, the ice.

★

It's the wire. They're caught deep in barbed wire, and can't get free. Can't get out of the water and onto the beach. They're waving their arms and screaming but the landing craft just goes over them, the propellers just cutting them apart.

★

In the snowstorm's gray, white and black
the only color is the traffic light:
its green and red
hard to see there at the night's edge.

Snow blanked the city, melting round the manholes
that plume with steam,
smoke from the engines of Hell.

★

'That cost me fifteen hundred bucks – same as an automobile –
but it'll earn itself back in five years.
It's the future.'
He banged on the side of the small walnut box above the bar
and the picture shivered back into frame.
'And I'll tell you this for nothing. It's the end of the movies.'

★

Ten below, and ice on the inside of the window.
Outside: the noise of dawn, another day beginning
without him. He wakes with one hand in the ashtray,
empty pockets and a buttoned head. Pigeons
riffling their feathers so loud they could be in the room.
All he's eaten since Friday is a fifth of Green River:
'The Whiskey Without Regrets'.
The neon sign is pulsing
and there's something in the corner but he can't tell what it is.
From his bed and the biscuity sheets
he hears an upstairs neighbor coughing,
smells cockroaches and poison,
sees where a rat's made a scrimshaw of the baseboard,
trying to get out.

★

In the Old Town bar, off Union Square,
he saw this bald guy in spectacles – staring at him in the mirror –
who turned and said: 'I don't see enough books, these days.
Good to find a young man reading. You work the docks?'
'How did you know?'

27

'The hole in your jacket shoulder. From the hook.'
His accent was thick, German-sounding,
curious eyes looming like fish through the glass.
'What do you do?'
'I make pictures. Just finishing up here: Mott and Grand,
West Houston. 18th Street today.'
'Maybe I've heard of you?'
He gave out something weird and foreign
with 'mac' at the end, and that's who he was.
'So, kid, you ever see *Brute Force*?'
'Yeah, that Captain Munsey . . . But . . .
you mean Lancaster, right? And De Carlo?'
'Let's not forget the lovely Ella Raines . . . Anyway . . .
Yes, well: the two of them are back in this new one. Together.
Burt and Miss De Carlo.
We start shooting in Los Angeles this spring.'
He goes over to the jukebox with a look on his face
and puts on the same song again: 'I'll Remember April'.
After a couple more drinks, a bunch of questions
about working the waterfront, he says:
'Look, Walker, I like you. You've got what we call
deep focus. Long eyes for seeing.
Here's my number out there. The name's Bob.'

★

*Nothing moved but the wind, nagging at the edges of the island. This was the
month of the great storm, when so many sheep died the shepherds built walls
with the carcasses, just to keep the snow from the few beasts left alive.*

★

28

The dust and litter
whipped round in circles, whirlpools
at the feet of the towers,
between the cliffs of buildings
he walks through: shadowed; lit;
shadowed; lit.
A ladder in the center of a maze
he climbs to see where he is,
where he went wrong.
From the top of the Empire State
the city fog like smoke after battle;
you can barely see the cannon,
the palisades, the armies massing,
just the black gorges, bluffs
and spiring towers of Manhattan.
But beyond the boroughs of New York
there were lights, now, and water
reflecting them, and he could see
that the city was finite after all.
Like the Cape Breton Highlands, the forest
stretched to the edge and stopped.

★

The old girl looked around the diner, then
leant over, conspiratorially.
He knew what was coming.
'It ain't the same, this place:
full of kikes an' spics an' niggers everywhere.'
'And me,' he said, getting up. 'But I'm leaving.'

★

He couldn't go back – not now,
not with this burning in him:
it would be like
climbing back into a vice.

If he stayed here
he'd end up in the East River, or Hart Island
with the stillborn, the nameless, the indigent dead.
He could feel the coal seam crackling underground.
He'd leave now. Tomorrow.
He'd try to get out.

★

Grand Central. Down below to the Oyster Bar
for a farewell dinner of Moonstones, Bluepoints, Wellfleets,
some littlenecks and cherrystones
and a plate of Malpeques from home – just there across the water.

A carton of Chesterfields for the journey, two quarts of Dundalk
and a one-way ticket out west – and that was him, cleaned out,
all he'd saved from a year on the docks.

The huge cathedral light angles down
– in long smoking buttresses –
from the starred blue ceiling to the concourse
and its information booth
ornate in marble and brass,
tiny as a pyx
or a jewelry box.

He waited in the light;
in the floating dust there
like the beam of a projector:
a still figure in hat and coat
with his old green army duffle bag,
among the traces of passengers, ghosts
passing through each other.
The flittering of the station-board
announcing platforms
with the flight of birds.

★

Ten minutes out
and it was like the moment your ears unblock.

He turned in his seat
to see the city appear,
suddenly behind him, ablaze.

1948

The ride west,
like his life, going by too fast
    – barreling through
        towns in the dark – trying to read
        each station's name –
or far too slow,
in the wastes of
Pennsylvania, Ohio,
dozing off and waking up with the same view
all day, still looking out on the same state
since whenever it was it got light.
But Chicago, when she came at last, looked beautiful, rising red
out of her lake, shimmering on that far shore.

Six hours to kill, he headed east
from the station, across the river,
and found LaSalle, for his next train, that night.
Checking his bag, he got some coffee, food,
watched the Midwest open up in front of him,
before he stood to stretch his legs
then kept on walking. It was the smell of the water.
And soon enough, there it was: the lake, like a sea
– going out farther

than Money Point to Newfoundland –
and all these pretty lights strung out along the bay.
Then he turned south to some gardens
and saw this water-spout like a whale-blow – this fountain,
like twenty humpbacks bubble-feeding,
breaching together, in a crown –
all lit from below, and the spray from it
wheeling white as the herring gulls up north.
Twelve hundred miles from here. Maybe more.

★

Aboard the 'Golden State': this red-and-silver streamliner
that would take him, in just three and a half days,
to another coast, a different ocean.

He slept from Bureau, Illinois, to Centerville, Iowa.
Prairie and plains. Prairie and plains.
He looked at his map, stared out the window.
Flat as hell for ten hours through the night,
all the way to Kansas City.
Kansas City . . . Lester Young and Coleman Hawkins,
Ben Webster, Charlie Parker. And all he could do
was wave out the window toward 18th and Vine.
The low moan of the train's horn in the night
calling back to the rows
and rows and rows of coaches,
a rhythm of breathing
held in a line there, rolling, long and slow.

★

Out walking, looking for signs: the first shoots of green in the trees round the lee of Lake Ainslie, and they'll be there — you just need to see. Stand still and listen, and you'll hear the silence fall back into shape; you'll hear the birds, you'll see the green.

★

Flat for days; clipping the top of Texas, into New Mexico,
the grass thinning to scrub; then dipping into Texas again
at El Paso, just after midnight,
across the Rio Grande to Arizona.
And the air had changed and the scrub thinned to desert,
the colors all red
along the border to Mexico
and he could feel the heat through the skin of the carriage
at Bisbee, where morning broke
and the ground rose
among the mine-workings,
and it looked like some frontier town out of a book.

★

You forget how it feels: the sun on your face. The heat drawing back in to the land. The land unclenching. The speckled alder and pin cherry, the spring birches in Strathlorne, each leaf distinct and clean as a green coin, new-minted.

★

Cactus started giving way to palm, crossing the Colorado
at Yuma, and into California at last: cutting north-west
with mountains on one side and a lake on the other,

39

its surface-glint like chainmail. He stared harder
and saw it wasn't water, but dead fish floating,
and the silver beaches weren't sand, just heads and bones.

An hour down the line, he saw grass. Green grass
in the desert; fairways and flags.
He's read about this. How,
impatient with Nature,
California just took control and built Palm Springs:
a resort for the rich and the old
to winter by their pools and play golf.
The Sonoran Desert
lapping at the edges of the green.
In this place, the sand-traps are the only things that are real.

Orange groves as far as you could see,
trees lined all the way to the mountains.
Then bulldozers rooting them up, levelling the ground.
Then the flat red scars.
Then the building work.
Then lines of tract homes all the way to the mountains,
grids of houses and roads –
and bright cars everywhere,
the moveable parts in some electric model of the future.
Clear, grade and pave, he heard it in the rails,
Clear, grade and pave.

★

And an hour of suburbs, before the public-address announcement
and the signs outside as it started to slow:

Welcome to Dreamland, Welcome to Wonderland,
Welcome to Hollywoodland. Welcome
to the City of Angels.

★

Pulling in to Union Station, he climbed down, unsteady,
like a sailor too long out to sea. The leaflets called it paradise
and they were right. He walked into warm sun, through gardens,
stands of orange trees, avocado trees, jacaranda, eucalyptus,
in to the concourse, clean and cool and high,
with chandeliers, and marble from France
and Belgium – the leaflet said –Vermont, Montana, Tennessee,
and out through a walkway of olive and pepper trees
to look back at it: a mission dressed with Mexican fan palms,
the bright gateway to a new future –
a new *American* future, it said – a paradise in the sun.

★

Across Alameda Street was a whole other country
– Chinatown – and Ferguson Alley was the door:
Hoysing Market, Si Chong, Soochow Restaurant,
but he settled for Jerry's Joynt on the corner,
a big plate of ribs, a cup of rye and a beer chaser.
He'd arrived. Somewhere.
Cloves, aniseed, ginger and cinnamon, paper lanterns
strung down the lanes in red and gold.
He'd done it: crossed America – sea to shining sea –
and he swallowed a mouthful of beer as a toast to himself,
took the whiskey nice and slow.

41

Ewan Ferguson, back east, would have loved this:
a street named after him.
Ewan, the kid he grew up with,
who lost three fingers down the mine
from rockfall, hasn't walked right
since a runaway cart went over his ankle,
lungs shot with silicosis,
who's never even crossed the Strait of Canso.
Never will.

He'll take the whiskey nice and slow.

★

What he needed now was a bed. With twenty bucks left
it was a rooming house or the mission, so he headed downtown
into Wonderland.

And there was City Hall,
just like in the movies but bigger, whiter,
lit up like God, and here was Main Street
stretching underneath it, block after block, in a smear of neon.
This was it. This was the city.
A magnesium strip; a carnival
on one long midway; a flaring
of something blank and feral, just unleashed
– panting on the sidewalk – ready to feed
off these hot, stinking bodies: drinking the light.

* LIQUOR * GIRLS * DANCING * CLEAN ROOMS * CHEAP EATS
* RIFLE RANGE * READ YOUR FORTUNE * MONEY TO LOAN *

BURLESQUE * 4 SHOWS DAILY * PENNY ARCADE * BEDS * BAR
* FOLLIES THEATER * COCKTAILS 15¢ * WE BUY SELL & TRADE
* DIAMONDS * BEER * MORE FOR LESS * GAYETY THEATER *
STAR THEATER * VACANCIES, $1 A NIGHT * BEER * JOYLAND *
DREAMLAND * DANCE-HALL * GIRLS * LIQUOR * VACANCY *

Six blocks of fairground, spilling out on the street: eyes
red as tail-lights, servicemen, longshoremen, oilmen,
Chinese, Japanese, Negroes, Filipinos, Mexicans, Indians,
even Hindus and Sikhs; streetcars, automobiles,
horns going; the panhandlers, streetwalkers, kids rolling drunks;
scuffles down the alleyways; saloon doors
swinging open to jukebox music
and a gash of laughter;
police cruisers; the calls of hot-dog sellers,
whispers from the pimps and the whores,
the dealers; the cops out on the corners,
the soldiers and sailors, their whistles, shouts,
broken bottles; reefer smoke, beer and sweat.
This was the city. Like Marseilles, perhaps,
or Casablanca. This was city life.
He walked for hours, up and down Main,
watching it flex and swell, feeling the crowd's edge
of fever and delirium, friction and threat: its black pulse.

He stopped in a bar and bought himself a ten-cent whiskey, then
figuring that an all-night picture-house was cheaper than a room
slid a quarter to the girl in the ticket cage and went in –
halfway through something good with Charles Laughton
and Ray Milland, then *The Naked City*
all shot in Manhattan, where he was on Tuesday

– was it *Tuesday*? –
Fulton Market, the El, McCormick's Bar,
the Williamsburg Bridge and the East River.
It looked hot as hell.
Felt like twenty years ago.

Most people around him were sleeping in their coats:
winos, the homeless, guys on the lam. The back row
was for couples, making out, thinking no one noticed.

He woke to the credits for *The Big Clock*,
saw what he hadn't seen, then slept some more.
He dreamt of France and the brigade getting stuck at Villons;
digging in, under tracer bullets all night long.
Together, under fire.
He missed all that, he realized; he realized he missed the war.
Looking around him, at the lonely deadbeats,
the drunks, he got up to go.

★

5.30, Sunday morning,
a man with a hose preceded him up Main Street,
fanning an aisle through the Styrofoam, food wrappers,
cigarette packets, torn shirts, snapped stilettos and the sour mulch
of broken glass, blood and butts and sick –
moving like a priest with a censer,
hosing the center down.

★

The rating with the bilge-bucket is swilling off the puke, and what was left of Joe McPherson who hadn't timed it right, his jump from the nets to this landing craft below.

★

Sunlight blooms in one window – five – ten – twenty – fifty – and the city was a field of standing light.

April, 48

★

So he went to the Union Mission.
They checked him over, gave him a meal of chicken, gravy,
mashed potatoes, a voucher for the Panama Hotel, E. 5th Street,
and some ideas for getting fixed up:
the address of the Labor Exchange,
where to pick up his twenty bucks a week from the GI Bill,
how you can eat for free at Clifton's on Broadway.

★

It was different in daylight. The taste of dust in the air;
The marshy smell of piss, spilt beer; the brown
stars of blood leading down the alleys.
Huge palm husks, lying there like twisted canoes.
Some people still staggering about,
some still drinking, others just folded in doorways.
Between 3rd and 5th, where the burlesques were,
he hardly recognized a thing in this thin, bitter fog:
signs switched off, shutters down.

45

He turned east at the Hotel Rosslyn, and past the King Edward,
and things got worse with every block. People sleeping out
under anything they'd got, or nothing at all;
blacks, whites, young and old, curled up on newspapers,
their bottles lined beside them, the rest in a gunny sack
or a cardboard suitcase or a paper bag.
The East Side. Skid Row.
And here, between Wall and San Pedro, the Panama Hotel.

'Welcome, my friend! Welcome.
I'm Billy, by the way. Billy Idaho.'
He was black, small and wiry, bright-eyed.
'I got a voucher.'
'I'm sure you do. You an ex-soldier, huh? Thought so.
Where d'ya serve?'
'Normandy, then Belgium, Holland.'
'Who with?'
'The North Novas, eh. How about you?'
'4th Infantry. Utah Beach. The first to land, they say,
but I didn't get as far as you. Sainte-Mère-Église is all;
got shot up good.'
'And welcomed home as a hero, I bet.'
'Yeah. Just look at us now: two heroes in a hostel on Skid Row.'
His eyes narrowed, changing his face.

'You know something . . .
The war made sense at the time:
all in black and white, good and evil, they said.
We came back to somewhere different
– those who came back at all –
every place full of people, all chasing something,

but no jobs for us, the guys who fought, y'know,
fought for freedom.'
He was pulling at the collar of his pearl-snap shirt,
'The women are in charge at home –
they're the ones who kept things going –
but the city's run by the combinations, or the Mob,
with City Hall and the cops in their pocket.
Money's all that matters. Money and the automobile.
And God's a roll of C-notes.
Gotta break free. Beat the system.'
Billy stopped talking then, suddenly worn out.

'So tell me about this city,' Walker said.

★

They walked for hours.

'This was always Skid Row. Always will be.
Just north of here's Little Tokyo,
called Bronzeville during the war.
Anyone halfway Japanese got sent to the camps in '42,
and the blacks came up from the South, looking for work
in the war industries, moved right in to those empty rooms;
eighty thousand, some say, sleeping in shifts –
hot-bedding in Bronzeville, it was called.
When the war was over, the jobs were over,
and the blacks moved south and the Japs were moved on.
Just like all the ethnics – all zoned out.
The Mexicans got pushed east and the Chinese north.
That's what they do here – demolish houses and build freeways.

47

It's the only city-planning there is – segregation.
And greed, of course.'

'So what brought you to Los Angeles?'
'You ever been to Idaho?'
'No.'
'Just potatoes and Mormons. White and cold.
And you're from Nova Scotia, I guess.'
'Cape Breton.'
'Colder *there*, I'm sure.

'So. Let's show you downtown.

'This is The Nickel – 5th Street from here to Pershing Square –
and these are our people: living free on the streets.
And this down here is Main. Where the fun is.'
'Yes. We've been introduced.'
'King Eddy's on the corner. Friendly bar.'
He was swinging around like a tour guide, pointing things out.
'And next is Spring Street – Money Street: banks and card-rooms,
gamblers, rich and poor.
Charlie O's over there, in the Alexandria;
that's another place to go.
And coming up is beautiful Broadway:
the Eastern Columbia, jewel of downtown,
all the great theaters, the top department stores,
they all run south of here
but we're going north.
The next block, between 3rd and 4th, you got Grand Central –
best market in town. Go there just before closing
and they're giving stuff away.
And get a load of this: the Million Dollar Theater. Some building.'

And then he stopped.
'Now: turn left at the next corner, look right up 3rd.'

He did as he was told. There was suddenly a big hill up ahead
with houses at the top – real houses – fairytale houses –
the mouth of a tunnel sliding underneath and what looked like
little orange railcars running up one side.

'That's Angels Flight, my boy, and *that* is Bunker Hill.'

★

They sat in a bar, watching the orange cars go up and down.
'You need to get things straightened out, son.
Gas. Food. Lodging. And a job, I guess.
How much cash you got?'
'Fifteen bucks.'
'Okay, you can get a week up on the Hill for six or seven,
and five'll get you fed. Not much money for gas, though,
so this one's on me.'
'Thanks, eh. I owe you.'
'What work can you do?'
'Apart from shooting Germans? I don't know,
I used to write stuff, before the war. I can do that.'
'What kinda stuff?'
'Oh, anything really. It comes easier than talking.'
'Newspapers? Could you do that?'
'Sure. I mean, yeah . . . I reckon I could do that.'
'Try the *Times*, or the *Tribune*. Not the *Examiner*.
I don't figure on you busting the Black Dahlia case.
Maybe the *Press*, though . . . Yeah,

you might get lucky with the *Press*.
Anyway, I gotta go. Take a look up the Hill. It's shabby
but it's got a heart. And you're way up on top of the city,
up above the smog and the dust.'

★

From here you could see right through
to the other side of the hill, where 3rd Street went,
or you could ride on the little incline railway
or climb the sets of stairs on either side.
He saved his penny and walked,
counting a hundred and forty steep steps to the top.
Rooming houses all the way,
the Hulbert, the Sunshine, the Hillcrest, the Astoria,
which all looked good enough, with decent rates.
Up top, on Grand and Bunker Hill Avenue, it was another world:
Queen Anne houses with turrets and cupolas,
wrap-around verandas, balconies, porches, arches
with painted balustrades, turned columns,
cedar-wood shingles,
fretwork, spindle-work, bays and oriels
with leaded windows and luminous stained glass.
Blurred and flaking, but beautiful still.
Few cars, so almost silent at times except for the cooing of pigeons.
A drugstore, laundry, market, café, delicatessen – and old folk
standing, talking on the street, like they're at home.
And then he felt a presence behind him. Turning round,
he saw the city, stretching out below.

★

There's an old photograph, of all my father's people ranked around his
grandfather and grandmother, tiers of dog-faced Victorians in rounded white
collars and black crinoline. So many breeds represented: Labrador, Newfoundland,
setters and spaniels. Long-muzzled, heavy-jowled retrievers all of them, even the
women, but, there at the bottom left, this human boy, my father, kneeling on a
tartan rug, four or five in his shorts, his shirt and tie, bewildered by this kennel
club of elders towering over him.

★

'So howdya make out, kid?'
'Pretty good. Got myself a bed for next week. On the Hill.
Well, the 3rd Street steps, anyway.
Looks okay for six bucks: a washstand and a hotplate,
use of the bathroom down the hall.'
'Now all you need is a job. And maybe a drink.'
'I brought this, eh. To say thanks. It's not Mount Vernon, but it'll do.'
'Sure will, neighbor. Sure will.
Got a couple glasses upstairs. C'mon up.'

'Say, Billy, you got a lot of books . . .'
'There's a lot of books to read.'
'I know some of these . . . yeah . . . some real good things here.
Oh, this one, I love this one – the Lowry, eh . . .
"You like this garden?" ' he recited, ' "Why is it yours?
We evict those who destroy."
. . . Anyway. Here's mud in your eye!'
Billy raised his glass to the younger man, and nodded.
'This garden's being destroyed right now.
The city's spreading faster than a man can walk,
chewing up the orange groves and dying from the center out.

51

Ten years, and downtown . . .
downtown will be strangled by freeways, I tell you,
because they're cutting off the circulation, killing the streets.
And it's not even a garden anyway, it's a desert,
and if you pulled the water it'd be a desert again.'
'I saw that on the train coming in, Palm Springs,
and there was this huge lake that was just dead fish . . .'
'Salton Sea – just salt and farm run-off, DDT.
It's the start of the tear – the San Andreas Fault –
that'll open us up, one day, like a can of beans.'
'Hey, Billy – have another drink.
You're right, though. I've only been here – what? –
a day, and I see all these gaps in the streets:
parking lots or just empty lots, like a bomb's fallen,
where it's just left like that, abandoned, going back to desert.'
'Well, Los Angeles was only a flag stuck in the sand –
they circled their wagons, built a camp
that became a pueblo, which became a city,
then a dozen cities sprawling to the sea.
But none of it's real, and nothing's *from* here. I'm not,
you're not, *nobody* is – not even the *palm trees* are from here –
the buildings are all just sets and stage-flats
because no one can keep up with the city.
Los Angeles is like a fridge or a car now,
it's built to break, so it's temporary.
When you get tired of your world you just *upgrade*.'
He blew out his cheeks and poured the last of the bottle.

'You're sure making me feel at home.'
'Just want to let you know what I know, kid, that's all.'
'I appreciate it, eh. I'll feel better, though, if I get a job.

How do *you* get by? You work?'
'Nah. I like to keep my head free, my body free.
'Sides, I want to read, talk to people, feel the sun on my face.
The mission looks after me, or I sleep on the streets.
You'll always find me round here, my friend,
and I hope you will. Now get some rest tonight.
Tomorrow you take the city.'

★

He cut out early the next day, said goodbye to the Panama
and started north, bag over his shoulder,
a haze on the city
that held in a chill from the night before, which he liked.
As he climbed, he could see it burning off the roofs,
lingering through the streets like smoke.

A rooming house on the 3rd Street steps, just there –
looking out on Angels Flight, the little railway –
sitting high over the tunnel's mouth, above Clay Street,
right next to the Hillcrest Hotel.
Monthly & Weekly Rates. Light Housekeeping.
Hot & Cold Running Water.
The Sunshine Apartments, it's called.
A halfway house; half way up Bunker Hill.

He dropped his bag off, washed and changed, then
headed back down, bought a coffee at the bottom,
at the Ferguson Café – which he took for good luck:
Ewan watching over him, all the way from home.

★

That time, in the half-light of morning, when I saw, up ahead, a black Labrador
pup squirming around with its legs in the air, then knew that the tail wasn't
right, that it wasn't a dog, but an otter: an otter, using the road as a scratching
post, brisking its fur before slipping back through the reeds to the pool, a skimmer
of light in the blue-black water.

★

'Have you worked on a newspaper before?'
'Well, sir, I was in the war . . .'
'Mr Walker, that's not really the kind of experience I meant.'
'I'm well-read. Well-traveled. And I can write.
I keep abreast of things.' And here he pulled out
City Development: Studies in Disintegration & Renewal
by Lewis Mumford, which Billy had given him as he left.
'Very impressive. Well. Let me see . . .
Perhaps we could give you a trial – unpaid, of course –
so we may discover if your . . . your *talents* . . .
meet the requirements, the high standards of the *Press*.
Miss Briggs – please take this gentleman up to Editorial
and ask if Mr Overholt is free.'

★

Everyone smoked, he was pleased to see,
but there were no sleeve-garters or eye-shades
or press-cards tucked into hatbands,
just the milling, the Brownian motion of people
all around, the noise:
the phones, the rattle of the Teletype – cross
between a sewing-machine and a drill – the clattering
and *ching* of twenty typewriters, the hiss

and rumble of pneumatic tubes, the shouts of 'Copy!'
He studied the editor, Overholt: the still point in a turning room,
saw his staff's deference, their devotion.
He flipped through back issues of *Life* and *Gourmet*,
looking at the pieces about the food and drink,
jotting down notes on what he saw around him:

No one was from here. The boss – Overholt – he's from back east, Pennsylvania, say, somewhere like Yough River: slow as a farmer, but sure and steady and smart. Distant memories of dust and smoke and seasoning, rolling tobacco, then the sweet notes emerging: a hint of milk and cookies. Closed at the start, there's depth and richness here: occasional tannins working against the sentimental to give a note that's sharp but never sour. A dry finish: rather restrained, but clearly solid, oaky, from a sound cask. Well made, well balanced, with some loss of liveliness; a sense of getting old.

★

'I'm Overholt. You wanted to see me?'
'Good morning, sir. Yes, I was wondering if you needed a writer.'
'What are your fields?'
'Well. I've traveled a fair bit. The Canadian Maritimes,
that's where I'm from; I know that coastline, down to Maine.
I signed up, trained in England, then fought in Normandy,
then on through the Low Countries. Germany.
After the war I worked in New York City for eighteen months
and now I'm here. I read all the time. Novels, history.
I'm interested in films and jazz. Cities.'
'Cities?'

'Yes. American cities.'
'What about American cities?'
'How they fail.'

'Hmm. Why don't we try you out on the City Desk, then, to start.'

★

'I'm Sherwood.'
'And I'm Rennert.'
'Good to meet you.'
'Let's get a coffee.'

★

They were talking about their work. The murders.
'The worst thing is finding them:
the way the bodies lie.
Never natural, you know? Legs
twisted up under the torso,
or splayed out, or kneeling.
The head, thrown back at the wrong angle.
Like they're dolls. Broken dolls.
One foot always missing a shoe.
One perfect hand, the other ground beef.
That the toes and fingers go black.
That the clothes sit so badly: the shirt open, skirts
rucked up, the hats tipped over the faces.
How they're still holding on to something
that might save them – their purse
or their newspaper or a dollar bill.
The way they soil themselves.

That there's so much blood in a body.
How quickly the dogs come.'

Then they stopped, and looked at him.
'What's your name again, pal?'
'Walker.'
'*Johnnie* Walker?'
'No. Just Walker.'
'Right. Let's take you round town.'

★

They drove a gray Studebaker, and he sat in back
watching the city open up outside, listening to them talk.
'So how's that new gal of yours?'
'Oh, man . . . I can get one on, just thinking about her.
Tall, pretty, great figure – I mean, *really stacked* . . .'
'You seeing her tonight?'
'Nah.' Rennert looked out the window.
'Why not?'
'Ah. Y'know,' he shrugged.
'Huh? You find yourself a real honey and you don't take her out?'
'It's just that . . .'
'Just what?'
'Well, I got a little tight last night . . .'
'And?'
'Some two-bit punk was hitting on her, and she didn't seem to mind . . .
Like she was . . . putting out, you know?'
'So what did you do?'
'Slugged him.'
'What did she do?'

'Chewed me out, then ditched me. Gave me the air.'
'Way to go, buddy. *Way to go.*'

★

The map of the city unfolded as they drove, and every day,
at every light or stop-sign he was noting down what he saw:
the theaters, bars and restaurants, hotels, stores,
bus stations, churches, banks and gyms, each street-corner
in every part of town.

North of the center was the highest land in the city limits,
Fort Moore Hill, and they'd been working on it
for years, Sherwood said, putting tunnels through it, digging out
the cemetery up top to look for Spanish gold.
Now it was blocking the 101, so it had to go.
This entire city was either being pulled down or built up.
They'd already started on the Harbor Parkway,
which would cut off the whole west side, north of Figueroa
three blocks away from Bunker Hill,
joining up with the Hollywood Freeway
to seal off two sides of downtown.
They stopped off there, one day, among bulldozers
and backhoes, cement trucks and cranes,
to get some shots of the progress,
but the pile-drivers . . . the hammer-drills . . . the blasting
from the building site . . .
the noise . . .

The noise of it, the noise of the guns, the heavy machine-gun fire, and nowhere to
hide and they were getting closer all the time and the flares were burning and the

noise was so loud, and all the shouting and the guns were going and now their 88s had found us, they'd found us out and were pounding our positions, pinning us down, pinning us, so many of us down.

He had his hands over his ears for twenty minutes,
even in the car, and they took it easy, driving round,
before stopping at a bar on 2nd and Spring,
near the *Press*, for a drink.

'You okay, buddy?' Sherwood slid him a shot of whiskey,
shaking out a smoke.
'Yeah. Thanks.'
'You were in the war, right? I've seen this happen before –
guys getting triggered off by something – crowds, sudden noise . . .'
'I'll be fine.'
'Yes, my friend – you better be. If you want the job, that is.'

★

The city's windows catch and flash the first sun, signaling to each other, it seems like: winking open, one by one.

People come to Los Angeles for refuge, sanctuary, but what they get is this massed, mechanized population moving in a confined space almost without collision or accident. The sounds, the movement of war: a ballet of battle without the guns.

When I went off to fight, Mother didn't know what to say, so she handed me a scarf.

May, 48

★

It was spring, but the wind was full of leaves. The roads were closed with broken
branches, fallen trees. I thought I heard the sound of a truck coming on, but it was
the storm again, gaining on me. My way was lit by the raw white gashes in the
sides of trees, the torn and opened bark. The ground was bright with lichen the
wind had stripped from the wood: gray, white, red and yellow in the dark.

★

He walked through Grand Central Market
with its blaze, its pyramids of fruit,
rubble-mounds of potatoes, sheaves of bananas
revolving on their hooks,
prickly pear, okra, eggplant.
He stopped to watch, at *La Casa Verde*, the watermelons
cleavered: falling open, rocking
slowly into still and perfect halves.
Melton's Meats had rows of joints, bacon, short ribs, heads – all
behind a bead-curtain of sausages –
ranks of sweetbreads, steaks, chops.
Scent-trails led to a soda fountain
for root-beer floats and malted milk; a Mexican stall
with *birria* burritos, tortas, chicken tacos;
Peerless Cheese and *Week's Poultry*
sharing a color-scheme of white, cream and gray.
Next door: stacked bags of dried fruit and candy,
trays of spices, burlap sacks of beans, pecans and pine-nuts,
and hanging above them, clumps of dried chilies
like lavish, papery, red-and-orange birds.
At the entrance, the sweet smells
of coffee, doughnuts, bagels, flapjacks.

From Stall A-1, *Grand Central Liquor*,
he picked out a pack of Luckies,
a bottle of Red Top and a brown paper bag.

★

Life at an angle, a 3:1 slope. Outside the window:
the palm trees, creaking in the breeze like doors;
Angels Flight, the funicular, the twin diagonal cars,
the moving diamonds
riding all day from Hill up to Olive, Olive
down to Hill, on *Olivet* or *Sinai*.
He eased the cork from the whiskey bottle
with the ceremonial . . . *ssspuck* . . .
and sat there, raising a glass to the slide.

★

We were running up the hill, zig-zagging like we were taught, when off to my
left I saw a sudden pink puffball, which was Cargill's head being coughed apart.

★

Coming to on his low, steel-framed bed: thin drapes,
a chair and table with a bowl for shaving, a mirror
with its glass split through.
His eyes are bad. He feels things
shift in the corners
but there's nothing there.
His stomach's in pieces.
The floor moves

and he thinks he sees rats running
right across the door.
There's two of something in the mirror.
His kidneys hum.
He turns on the light and the whole ceiling's crazed
like old pottery. He blinks, looks again.
The cracks all gone.
The night's drained out of the sky, and it starts over.
The bottle's lying on its side
but there's still a drink in it.
The cockroaches watch from the walls.

★

He went down to Clifton's for some split pea soup;
chili and beans,
corned beef hash if he could.
The line was long at the glass counter, but it moved quick.
HELEN was his helper of the day.
She readjusted her weight at the servery,
breathing heavy, a dampness in the creases round the neck,
the ladle like a teaspoon in her hand.
Heaping his plate with brown mush,
she grinned through tiny teeth, 'Growing boy, ay?'
and winked. The eye lost in its brittle pleats.
Then to her mouth again: the tongue
was moving over the lips,
moistening, back and forth, re-applying.
The tray seemed small
as he slid it down the rails to the cashier, nodding at the sign
NO GUEST NEED GO HUNGRY FOR LACK OF FUNDS

before shuffling on, ashamed, to the darkest corner,
behind the plastic redwoods and the waterfall, to eat.

★

*The soft lands of the Margaree, the flats, the river-meadows, thick with trout you
could catch with your hands as they lay still under the ledges, gazing upstream.
Reaching for the most tentative touch, just there above the tail, then gently up
under the belly till it accepts your hand and you can rock it in the water, back
and forth, lulling it easy.*

*Difficult after that, to pull it up by the gills: to kill it and clean it and open it
out on the fire, but you will.*

★

He couldn't sleep nights. So he walked.
A different route each time, just to pay attention.
South along Olive, past the rows of frame houses
toward the giant neon signs – the Richfield Tower's oil-well
pumping black gold on 6th and Flower,
the Church of the Open Door
with its lettering on the roof reading **JESUS SAVES** –
to the Biltmore and the dark of Pershing Square
– the rustle of men, busy among the palms and bamboo.
Along Clay, down 2nd to Main and all the way to City Hall;
down 6th to Broadway and its theaters: the Los Angeles,
the Palace, the Orpheum, the Globe.
Or he'd stay up on the Hill, on its highest point
on Grand, near the Dome Hotel, or the benches
over the 3rd Street Tunnel,
and watch the lights of the city guttering below.

The streets and stones held the heat of the day
as the palms turned to silhouettes in the silver-blue of evening.
He noticed bats, flaking their way
across the rooftops, over the air-conditioning units;
the neon blade-signs below
clicking like bug-zappers, sparking through the night.

It was four one morning when he saw it through the rain
– the coyote – nosing out of the Spring Arcade onto Broadway,
slinking down the asphalt: suave, long-limbed, eyes
dabbed with neon
from the theater signs on either side,
then disappearing down the blind alley behind the Roxie.
He went in after it. Nothing.
He would see it again on Cinnabar Street, or Lebanon,
on Sack Alley, in the vacant lots below Hope, between 7th and 9th,
or flickering up from the Hill Street Tunnel: yellow eyes
like headlights.

★

He got the job: cub reporter on the *Press*
at twenty bucks a week. Working the City Desk
with Sherwood and Rennert. Anything else, after hours.

★

'You know, Walker, it's not like in the movies.'
Sherwood was eyeing him steady in the rear-view mirror.
'What?'
'Los Angeles. Y'know, the beautiful woman
turning up in your office, unannounced. The cigarette girl,

the hat-check girl, the waitress in the diner,
the singer in the bar downtown.
And it's not about private eyes, the gun in the desk drawer,
bottle in the filing cabinet, the body on the bed,
body on the floor, a hole in the body, holes in the wall.
It's a mess. And not a pretty one.'
'I can see.'
Sherwood was just about to start over when a black-and-white
braked and turned, hitting the siren, squealing off south.
'Let's go.'
They were eating up Broadway and spitting it out:
3rd, 6th, 8th, 12th, till they slid to a stop
behind the cops, in a driveway, jumping out
and going after them, round the side of the house,
where the pool was lit, deep blue, with dancing spots and long
streams of aquamarine
– like the back of a kingfisher, he thought –
and a body resting on the bottom.
He stood watching as the flashbulbs went,
as Sherwood talked to the cops;
the kid was five or six maybe,
a ribbon of red
floating up between its legs.

'C'mon, we're going,' Rennert said.
'LAPD lock-down. This is a Mob house.'

★

*Finding the otter's slide, then seeing it, suddenly, nosing across the pool, its wake
a turbulence like silk twisted round a blade. Your eyes tune to the shape of birds,*

and you see them everywhere: the kingfisher's flash, the wing coverts of a jay.
There are spokes of light through the dark pool.

★

He walked the monochrome world of the city, after hours,
in the dissipating heat
watching his shadow feed in front of him, tightening
under the streetlight, sidling up each wall
then folding into it, bending like a stick
slid into water.

★

'Hey, stranger! Yeah, you.
Why'n hell you standin' there, drinkin' on y'r own?'
'Beats me.'
'Well . . . ain't that the *damnedest* thing,'
she looked around, astonished.
'Handsome here don't know why he's drinking!'
His smile didn't reach his eyes: 'I know why I'm drinking.
Just don't know why I'm here.'
'You must be a few cents short of a dollar, honey,
'cause this *here* is the City of Angels, Tinseltown, *sit-yoo-ated*
in the Land of the Free and the Home of the Brave.'
'Yes. Los Angeles,' he looked at the sweat patches
in the dress a size too small, the paste jewelry, the caked mascara.
'A few improvements wouldn't hurt, here or there.'
'The hell y'driving at? Look, sugar, you're cute as all get out,
so let's give this another shot.
What say we go to my hotel, get acquainted?'

66

'I don't think so. Thanks all the same.'
'Don't give me no brush-off. C'mon, let's highball outta here!'
'I'd say you've had too many highballs already.'
'The *nerve*.'
'Beat it, sister. Go on, dust.'
'Hey, Johnny! This guy's putting the bite on me!'

A crash as Johnny goes down, the table with him,
the door slamming shut.

★

There was a new face at the paper.
He'd started at the bottom, in the classifieds,
then swung a job as copy-boy on the *Press*: gopher, dogsbody,
running copy to the subs, running for the editors
and for Mr Overholt, the boss.
He watched this kid –
tall and very pleased with himself, clicking his pen,
always moving, hanging round each desk,
learning to wave his sheaves of carbon-paper
just like the big boys.
He wouldn't leave old Overholt alone, unctuous
over each sentence, each page design: his voice,
his laugh, louder every day.

He watched this kid very carefully, taking notes:

> They call him Pike, short for Pikesville, where he's from: lean,
> swaggering and clearly young, no time spent in the wood. An
> unusual oily top-note, close to fish- or bicycle-oil. Too pushy
> on the palate: smooth, but with no complexity. So smooth, in

fact, as to be almost slippery. Loud, full of brag, but strangely thin and artificial: chemical notes of turps, film-cases, acetone. Started sweet then dried fast, turning astringent. Immature, so the finish is hot and short and bitter: like sucking on a dime. Assertive, but with no real personality, no balance or integrity. A lightweight needing a great cask and some depth: any kind of character.

★

Billy was hard to find, but there he was
in the King Edward, 5th and Los Angeles,
sitting up at the bar with a book.
Walker hung his hat, and sat up at the next stool,
tapping out a couple Camels. 'Drink, Billy?'
Billy grinned with his big strong teeth, 'Could use a straight shot.'
The barman set them up, and they raised their glasses:
'To Nova Scotia!'
'Idaho!'
'So – how's the newshound? Putting the world to rights?'
He was pretty ripped already, but that was fine.
'Yeah, it's good. I'm getting to know this place, eh.'
'Not like home, I bet? Bit livelier?'
'Everything's livelier than Inverness County.'
'You got a girl back there?'
He wasn't expecting that, but he rallied: 'Used to.
Don't know now.'
'Hard to keep them, ain't it. After what we seen.'
It all just flooded in then, and he talked and talked
about the flashbacks and tinnitus, the hearing loss and panic attacks
and how he'd flipped at the building site.

The way he held himself together like a piece of glass.
'I used to have a family of two hundred men, a company,
and we were all we had. Watching each other's backs.
And after that, I'm lost. I'm fucking lost.'

★

They talk about the city as this place to get on, meet people, have fun,
but sometimes it just feels like a labyrinth: that old game of survival
and loss.

People keep saying the Mexican border's only a couple hours away. Like
that makes everything OK.

June, 48

★

He saw film-crews all the time around the Hill:
Angels Flight, Clay Street, Grand Avenue, the drop down 2nd
from the Dome to the Hotel Northern.
They were shooting in the 3rd Street Tunnel one night
and he stood around, watching a guy run through, shouting,
toward the cameras, again and again till they got it right.
He found out the name of the director – something strange
like 'Cinnamon' or 'Sinnerman' and went back
to look for that scrap of paper, and the number he wrote
five months ago in that bar with the tin ceiling
on 18th Street, in New York City in the snow.

'*Zinnemann*. Fred Zinnemann. Friend of mine. From back home.
Who'd you say you were again?
Oh, right . . . Yeah . . . Yeah . . . Ah, yes – the young man from the docks.

69

I remember. And you say you're here? In *Los Angeles*?
In Bunker Hill. Hm. Well, we're there on . . . let's see . . . Tuesday.
We shoot in the afternoons. Best light for this one.
It's the 200 block, North Hill Street. Come over and say hello.'

So, it's the other side of the Hill Street Tunnel,
between City Hall and what's left of Fort Moore Hill.
He goes down Court Street and sees cameras rigged
above the north end of the tunnel, where it opens onto Temple,
shimmering and doubling
in the midday heat; people standing round vans,
eating sandwiches, drinking coffee, and there he is, he's sure:
glasses glinting under a panama hat, laughing with the crew
below an electric fan and a board that reads CRISS CROSS.
'My friend from New York!' he says, walking over. 'You made it.'
'Yes, sir.'
'We're on a break. Let's go to my trailer.'

Throwing his hat down, he turns on the gramophone:
'*This lovely day will lengthen into evening*
We'll sigh goodbye to all we ever had . . .'
'Drink?'
'Yeah, sure. Whatever you're having.'
'Lemonade. But I've whiskey if you want it.'
'Please.'
'Worked out okay, that last one. *Cry of the City*.
It's opening soon, couple months.
This one, though – this one's *special*.
Lancaster and Duryea. Amazing. And De Carlo:
seems she can really act. We're shooting her now.
And so what brings you over to California? The sun?'

70

Walker had forgotten the clotted German accent.
'Just got a job, eh. Reporter at the *Press*.
Y'know, it seems there's a movie made every day in this town.
It's like one big open-air film-set.'
'Great diagonals. These old houses – all the hills!
And perfect at night – the angles you can get.
I remember we talked about that in New York, no?
There was a guy working here last month:
cinematographer, name of Alton. He's the best.
He calls it "painting with light". How about that?'
'I like it. Say, didn't he do *T-Men*? And that new one
that's just opened . . . *Raw Deal*?'
'That's him. That's him – works with Tony Mann.
They were shooting this chase scene down in the storm-drains.
I saw the rushes. Unbelievable sequence –
one light on a dolly and the rest
just police torches. This *cube of light*, y'know,
moving through the tunnel like an elevator car.'

He went silent. Walker sipped his drink. That tune again,
'. . . *Alone where we have walked together*
I'll remember April and be glad.'

'I might be doing something on your old waterfront.
Corruption, you know, like we talked about.
There's a guy writing on it now,
doing pieces in the *New York Sun*. Interesting.
Anyway. I got to get back to work. Stay and watch.'
On a chair was a jacket with something written on the back:
PRONOUNCED
SEE-ODD-MACK

And there she was, parked up on the slope
in her Ford convertible, sunglasses, spotted dress.
Children playing in the background, old ladies
strolling down to Temple; then this creepy blond guy
dressed like a kid, running, throwing a ball
to a terrier that chases, barking, after him. Over and over.
Stands outside the steps to the house
watching her, again, over his shoulder,
as she walks up the stair slowly;
it's a scene that never ends:
he's tossing the ball in the air, again and again,
as if he's been here on this street
doing this since he was a boy.

★

Heat on the island made those weeks of summer frantic, desperate with life, but
nothing to do but get away, walk to Lake Ainslie – fish for trout if the flies and
clegs would let me – or climb that red oak, up over Loch Ban, and hang in my
tree like the sun.

★

It's getting hotter every day, but after work
up on the Hill, there's a breeze,
and he buys a paper from the one-armed man
who's always there in his suit, with one sleeve
pinned up, at his news-stand in the shade
of the pharmacy on 3rd and Grand.
Getting a Coke from the cooler outside the Nugent
he goes to sit on the benches, their green paint flaking in the sun.

Old men were out, on corners, watching the world,
stroking cats and dogs, chatting, picking up scraps of litter
and looking at them, directing trucks as they reversed.
Making themselves useful. Part of this city, still.

People nodded to him now in the neighborhood, knew his name
in Budget Basket, in the drugstore or the bars:
the Angels Flight Café where he'd go to read,
or the night place, Los Amigos, across the street.

The old man going past is half-folded. Right-angled
as a wall-bracket, he walks south every day
down Bunker Hill Avenue to the Public Library,
staring at the ground.
He can look both sides, but not ahead, and never up.
The pleasure of sitting must be immeasurable.

The only thing that moves, all day, is the sun,
and you tell the time by its slow shadows.
Dogs are stretched out in the heat, breathing loosely.

He reads, sometimes, out on the porch of the Sunshine Apartments,
the open wooden framework of verandas and breezeways,
gazing through the palms across the rails of Angels Flight
to the walls and windows of the Hulbert, another SRO.

The paper was full of weather, the hottest summer in twenty years,
its pages, turned in his hands, going sun-dried and brittle.
Robert Mitchum getting busted
over there in the Hollywood Hills.
And up behind, in the San Gabriels, they're saying

it's so dry and still
you can hear the mountains hum. 'Fire-weather', they call it.

★

At the *Press*, Pike is everywhere,
nodding his head on its neck
like one of those balsa-wood dragons with strings
you see down in Chinatown,
nodding hard,
harder when Overholt looked in his direction,
nodding in that dismissive way that said:
Yes, yes, I know. I knew that *long ago*.

When he's particularly pleased with himself
he splays out on his chair
till he's almost lying on it, legs and arms out
like the world's too small for him.

★

They found Captain Stewart next day, propped up against a tree and thought he
was sleeping, till they saw that most of the other side of him was gone. A plump
arm lay next to him, the stuffing coming out of one end.

★

'Make it a beer.'
In this heat, Craby Joe's was a small steambath inside a bigger one.
The guy next to him was staring, blankly,
riddling his ear with a pipe-cleaner.

74

He'd had some kind of a stroke
and his face dragged down on one side, like it had
missed a button.
He said, 'Mighty hot,' to no one in particular,
then ducked to lip at the straw in his bottle of Star.
Lifting his head carefully, he looked around,
tongue flitting out like a lizard's, tasting the new air:
'Santa Ana's coming. The fire-wind!'

'Hey, fella – buy a lady a drink?'
Walker nodded without turning.
'That's swell of you.'
She pulled a pack of Parliaments out of her purse
and he saw the tag-ends of dinner at her mouth, thoughts
passing over her face
like a drift of cloud-shadows over the land.
He switched back to his empty bottles, the whiskey in his hand.
'You look lonely, soldier. How about my place?'
'No thanks.'
The smell of greasy cosmetics. Refried beans.
'What's eating you?'
'Nothing.'
'C'mon, sweetheart, just a little fun . . .'
'Take a powder, would you?'
'Hey, don't get sore. You a fruit or something?'
She turned to the pipe-cleaner man.
'Howdya like that? This fairy should be in the Waldorf
or the Crown Jewel, not a decent place like this!'
'That'll do, sister,' said the bartender: 'Scram.'
Walker got up, slapped down some change,
bending over her

and whispering something as he picked up his hat and left.
Her mouth went square, and she started to howl.

★

He couldn't remember the last time he'd been touched.
The sign said:
`Palm-Reading. Chinese Medicine. Happy Massage.`
There were jars of leaves, grains, twisted roots,
the sweet smell of almonds, sesame oil and candles.
She wasn't young, or pretty, but had a smile at least.
She worked his back like a washboard, quick and hard –
'You ver' tired, da'lin', ver' tired,'
releasing the braided muscles before slowing, going
farther down. 'Scuse me, mistah. Turn over, please.
You want more, da'lin'?
You like hand, or whole way?'

★

Letting the night loosen around him
he wandered slow down 6th, past Cole's,
past the Greyhound station,
till he reached the East Side,
turning off down Maple, Winston, Pedro, Crocker.
In each dark corner, the whites of their eyes;
every hand stretched out.
The nickels and dimes he spilled
into their open palms
were soundless, thin as
water in this heat,
evaporating

76

as he walked away.
Men sitting round bottles, shifting in their rags, eyes
watching the lights of planes drift overhead.
Men lined up, with their kit, sprawled out on the sidewalk
in rows, wearing too many clothes,
wearing all their clothes,
trying to get some shut-eye before it all starts over.
Trying all they could.

No sign of Billy anywhere.

Only a prowl car, slewed in
to the corner of 4th and Los Angeles,
revolving lights like some carousel, and two cops running,
yelling, '*Stop – police!*' at this guy
who's already through 3rd
and halfway down the block to St Vibiana's.
He pulls up,
steps away from the dark, spreading
his hands: taking the shape
of a standing star.
He might have been shouting,
but he was too far off to make any sense.
Then suddenly he reaches for his top pocket
and seems to pull out a red handkerchief,
steps backward,
faltering,
then rips another one
right out of his face.
It was only then that Walker heard them,
the sound of the shots.

After that, he kept going north,
past the beacon of hope, the flood-lit stone
towering above,
over all the human debris, poor as dust – all these winos, con-men,
crooks and cops, pimps and streetwalkers –
the raised hand of the law:
the whited sepulcher of City Hall.

And on to Alameda and Chinatown
till he found the path that climbed to the Stone Quarry Hills
up through fields and houses of the new pueblo to the high ravines,
Chavez, Sulphur and Cemetery, Solano and Reservoir,
to Mount Lookout in between.
And he stood there, far over City Hall –
over the lights of Los Angeles –
as if the whole sky and all the stars had fallen:
displayed, spread out below
in a flickering maze,
this bed of moving embers.

★

*The ledged raven cries out, cricks open the pages of his black book, twice, and is
off: already reading the sky, the land that runs under him.*

★

Christmas and New Year had been and gone,
and there was his friend, on San Julian, still wearing a Santa Claus hat,
helping an old lady with her home of pallet and tarp.
'Billy?'
He looked up, 'O . . .' his hand to his chest, '. . . *Can-a-da!*

78

With glowing hearts we see thee rise! How's tricks?'
'Time for a coffee?'
'Sure . . . Just let me get Velma fixed up here.'
Velma gave a little wave, then stood smiling,
in her suit of flies,
holding tight to her pocketbook,
both hands rashed with raised red dots,
the nails cracked white and open.

'See, it's all about *functionality* now,
which is speed, efficiency and profit.
They call it *a clean sweep*
to eradicate *crime* – which means blacks – to fumigate
and disinfect the city against *disease*
– which means the black and the poor –
to demolish *slums* and *blighted areas* – which means
the homes and communities of the black and poor and old.'
Billy took another mouthful of coffee, looked up at Walker:
'They call this *progress*, when it's really only greed.'
A cop car careened past, siren going.
'At least in the war there was some common purpose –
in the same boat, all in it together, y'know?
Now here we are, in our own country,
scrambling over each other, just
trying to stay afloat.'

He scrutinized the table for a while,
started picking at the label of a ketchup bottle.
'You got a girl – here, I mean? Young guy like you . . .
You've been away a long time, it's only natural, y'know?'
He went back to working on the label.

79

'I know what the war does to men, but you can't let it win.
You can't let it kill all the good things inside you.
After all these years. It's over now. It's really over.'
He tipped his hat back and looked out the window:
'Nearly morning. Gotta get some sleep.'

★

*Her body clambered mine, climbed me like a flame; Christ, I loved her: all
through the night, helping her over the edge:* Oh God, *she's calling,* I'm going
over, I'm going over now, and I'm falling   falling   falling

★

He woke to the cats coming home, and there was a pinkness
in the dawn light he recognized, a cleanness in the air.
He parted the blind, and there was snow on Angels Flight,
and when he got out in it, snow
from Bunker Hill all through downtown. Los Angeles was white,
white as City Hall.
And he felt it again, that heat inside him: the road.
Burning like a coal seam underground.

★

When I went to war, they gave me a travel Bible with a zip, with my
name inscribed on the flyleaf: *from his loving Father and Mother.*

Like deer, you'll never see me, I thought to myself: just a glimpse,
perhaps, on the way to being gone.

February, 49

★

80

Saturday night bled into morning and he walked west,
and he'd keep walking till he reached the sea.
Staying clear of the freeway, 10th became Olympic Boulevard
and in a couple of hours he could make out, up on the right,
what he knew was Mount Lee,
and the big, beat-up, white sign
hanging in the darkness:
what lights that were left on it, flashing up in segments –

OLLY   **WOOD**   **LAND**

– then all together as **OLLYWOODLAND**.
He was passed by an A-frame on wheels, heading west
towed by a truck.
The smell of orange blossom on a Sunday morning
in the dead streets of Los Angeles –
the Spanish-style courtyard apartment complexes,
Mediterranean villas with arrow-loops, Mexican ranch houses
with minarets, Swiss chalets with fire-pits and pools,
Medieval-style, Prairie-style, Beaux-Arts-style –
stretching in its long straight lines down to the gray Pacific Ocean.
Beyond Hollywood and Beverly Hills
they're still building: identical new bungalows, thin
as stage-sets or show homes,
landscaped in spilt paint, spreading west.
Wet streets: red splashes of light, then green –
and then green all the way to the sea.

★

The green lights through the dawn, guiding our way through the mines, across the
Channel to France. The lines of our boats, as far as you could see.

★

The Pacific. Light rain pitting the sand at Santa Monica
as he kept walking, over the long empty beach, to the water's edge,
left his clothes in a pile
and walked on, into the sea.

Warmer, in February, than the Atlantic ever is. *The smell of it.*
It was funny: none of his people could swim.
He learnt in England
those years before the landings, and loved it now.
Rocked by the sea's currents. The freedom.
They'd never believe he was here,
swimming in the ocean in winter.

Underwater, you hear the current moving,
redistributing the pebbles:
the sound of fat on a hot skillet.

★

The chintz and antimacassars, the china figurines crowding the window-sills, all
colors faded to pink, pale blue; photographs of the dead, slipped sideways in their
mounts; the dining-room 'kept for best', cold as the tomb and never entered; the
smell of wet ash, the gloom of gas-lamps.

★

After the five hours walking, he swam
till his legs were lightened,
his head clear from feeling nothing.
Brown pelicans, diving for fish:
like short-falling, graceless gannets.

There were clam-diggers on the foreshore,
some early yachts in the sweep of the bay
and he could see men fishing far out at the end of the pier
beyond the funfair and the dance-hall,
like the quays back east at Chéticamp, Inverness and Margaree,
down to Finlay Point and Mabou:
blue silhouettes at the edge,
still watchers of the moving sea.

★

*The locals crumping through snow to see which boat had put in. The frozen
harbor like a terrible accident: as if some ballroom's chandeliers had fallen, leaving
smashed shards of inch-thick ice: this impossible puzzle laid out as plate glass –
a blank jigsaw with a million pieces.*

★

*The sea opened its arms to us, unconditionally. Welcoming us all to the deep, each
to our own hole in the water.*

★

The carnies are waking. They've been sleeping on benches,
or under the pier, and are moving around.
One wanders over, shoes too big for her feet,
home-made tattoos under a stained vest – grinning,
with no front teeth, lighting
one cigarette off another and saying:
'It's real quiet here, out of season. Real quiet.'
She looked back at the Big Dipper, the carousel, the Ferris wheel.

83

'I had a good life, y'know? Home. Kids. A proper life.
I just slipped a bit.'
She examined the sand, closely.
'I just slipped.'

★

He took a Red Car back.
The papers showed Mitchum, mopping out his cell.

★

He remembered the lieutenant with shell-shock, walking round and round in tight circles, throwing his head back, moving his hands like he was knitting.
The dying men watching, each marked on the forehead with an 'M', meaning they'd been dosed with morphine.

★

February on the island was the wolf-month, or the dead-month, which the sailors prayed would begin with a heavy storm and end in calm, with hope of spring –
come in with the head of a serpent, go out with a peacock's tail.

★

The next day: Pike
on some street corner, measuring the length of his spit.
Pushing back his flop of hair,
narrowing his eyes at the middle distance; swaggering, smirking.
A forest of tics.

84

Pike would go far:
the looks of John Dall in *Rope*,
the moral integrity of George Raft.

Pike snapping the lid of his Zippo, clicking it
up and down, up and down,
as if to illustrate his restless intelligence –
restlessness, at least, that he hadn't, in the past hour,
put his foot on a new and higher rung of the ladder.
He sprawled on his chair,
unable to adequately contain his long legs
and huge clown-like shoes,
looking around for some fresh advantage:
click, click, click.

★

He caught up with new movies he'd missed since the fall:
the one Siodmak told him about, with the storm-drains –
He Walked by Night – and the one he'd watched being shot
in the 3rd Street Tunnel. It was Van Heflin he'd seen, and there he was
running right down the steps by the Hillcrest,
then along Clay Street under Angels Flight.
Criss Cross, though, was better still.
He'd shot all over Bunker Hill, in bright daylight, and one scene
right inside his own building: the lobby and stairwell; his own door.
That tune, 'I'll Remember April', playing again.
Reminding him of what women are like:
'You always have to do what's best for yourself,' she said,
'You just don't know what kind of world it is.'
'Well,' he replied, 'I'll know better next time.'

★

He took a drink that night: sat, dulled by beer, sharpened,
cut through by whiskey.
An inch of ash on his cigarette;
the beer-mat in shreds.
He saw the women, dressed and coiffured,
made-up like the dead,
practicing their expressions in the backbar mirror,
then trying them out on him.
He stood up, walked out of the frame.
He'd come to know, over time, to only watch
what women hide,
not what they show.

★

He'd go down Central, maybe:
see who was playing at the Last Word
or Club Alabam, or the Dunbar, or the Downbeat – where
one week in March he heard Dexter Gordon and Teddy Edwards,
Mingus with Buddy Collette –
or once at Lovejoy's where he sat two tables from Art Tatum,
just watching his hands. Always alone at the piano, with a beer,
a cigarette in the ashtray, smoke
twisting up to the spotlight
tight as rope.
No one ever sat in. Not with Tatum.
And no one could follow him.

★

The paper for March 31st showed Mitchum released after sixty days.
A much smaller piece, buried on the back page, wrote that Caleb Hill,

86

a 28-year-old black chalk-miner from Wilkinson, Georgia, had been
taken from the county jail the day before, and lynched. An unnamed
local resident was quoted, explaining, 'It's just a Negro.'

★

He'd got to know more people at the *Press* –
who'd been there as long as the boss, and all from out east like him:
Templeton from Iowa's an okay guy,
well-bred, sense of humor, smart,
and May Wood from Boston, the face of the paper.
Some said she's a dyke, but he didn't think so
and he liked her anyway – liked to make her laugh.
The rest were harder going.
The compositors and proof-readers
looked up at him with the eyes of ruminants: carefully,
without movement. If something required scrutiny
there was a slow, elaborate shift of the shoulders. The stare.
Rennert and Sherwood were his team, in their cheap suits,
three-day shirts and stained ties,
keeping him straight on the city:
the organized crime, the stoolies, bent cops and politicians,
the Mob bars, queer bars, the bars for Mexicans, Indians, Chinese,
the ninety-six clubs, hash-joints, card rooms, cathouses.
They knew the city from Griffith Park to the harbor at San Pedro,
from Pasadena to Malibu, Point Dume.
They smoked full-time, traded girls like baseball cards,
wore their hats tipped back,
had a bad word to say about everyone, told stories
even they didn't believe.

And then there was Pike:
holding up the stacks of manuscript pages
and tapping them down on the desk to align them,
patting them straight at the top and the sides.
He looked around – stretching, spreading his knees wide –
made a noise in his throat,
then another; he was starting a new laugh.

★

He was used to his room at the Sunshine: walls
lined with brown paper, the all-night
fidget and fuss of the air-conditioning, the mice
scuttering in the ceiling space.
He'd bought a red geranium in a pot, for the table by the window.

The dust falls everywhere, filling the long sunbeams
with its gray sift; collecting in the glasses, the ice-trays,
so every drink swims with it. He could see it, when he held
his whiskey to the light, hanging there
and drifting to the bottom, where it didn't matter anymore.

★

He met a girl one night in Los Amigos, young and beautiful.
Long black curls. Said her name was Gitana,
said she wanted the world.
She was new in town, so the next day they went walking
and he showed her his neighborhood, the trees in their fall colors,
all his favorite streets and houses around Grand
and Bunker Hill Avenue: the Castle, the Melrose,

the Brousseau house, the Heindel house, the Dome.
He waved to Mr Mellon, in the pharmacy, said hello
to the red-haired, one-armed newspaper man;
pointed out Dr Green's surgery.
She shrugged, talked about Olivia de Havilland, Betty Grable,
Cary Grant and Spencer Tracy,
how she wanted to be like them: a star.
She was the loveliest thing. She was sixteen.

He told Sherwood about her the next day, in the car:
'Of course she's beautiful,' he said. 'She's sixteen.
Everyone's beautiful when they're *sixteen*.'

★

One night, round Thanksgiving, the old lady downstairs
was standing at her door, holding a shoe-box.
'Alfredo not well. He *real bad* this time.'
He saw a shriveled animal on its side,
a hamster perhaps, eyes like raisins.

★

He gave himself a cat for Christmas, just a dollar and a half,
black all over, more for company than killing:
Margarita Carmen Dolores;
Rita for short.
He loved watching her, decanting herself
in one pulse
from the window-ledge to the floor.

★

89

The paper said he could try out on movie reviews,
so he went to see *Deadly Is the Female* in the Cameo, or the Star,
one of those theaters next to the Arcade.
He thought about it all night. That long take
inside the getaway car: one shot that lasted three minutes easy
and was just real life, right there.
It made sense of some things, how you get caught up in stuff,
like the guns, when he says, 'I feel good when I'm shooting them.
I feel awful good inside, like I'm somebody.'
But the guy can't kill, and the woman wants to.
It's his shame, in the end, his disgust – up against her desire.
He went back the next evening, and the night after that –
this time with Gitana. She kept lighting cigarettes,
looking around the theater, studying the audience.
She squeezed his arm at the credits;
said she preferred musicals, actually.

★

Valentine's Day, and he was covering a boxing night
down at the Olympic, over on 18th & Grand.
Even he'd heard of Bolanos, out of Los Angeles
by way of Durango – the city's favorite fighter –
and they were already booing the other guy, Art Aragon – slight,
showy, all dressed in gold: gold trunks, gold robe.
'Alright, ladies and gentlemen, here we go: twelve rounds . . .'

Inside the din and darkness,
in this box of light, two men
trying to get out alive,
hit each other harder,
and the crowd, roaring

90

at the white cage,
the roped net holding
men, fighting,
in a stall, a stockade of harm, a cell —
a pin-point, spot-lit diorama.

★

From the table, he picked up the pink rose
he'd bought last week for Gitana.
It shattered in his hand.

★

There was the sharp
stink of disinfectant;
ash-barrels on fire,
throwing up flakes of light
by which he could see them:
rows of them, each face
creased with age and heavy use
and beginning to rub, to open
at the seams, like an old map.

'Here we are,' said Billy, under his breath.
'I've told them about you, how you want to help —
how you want to tell their story.'
Clearing his throat, he steps into the light.
'Evening, everyone. I've brought a friend.
A roll-call, gentlemen, if you please.'
From the blackness he saw their eyes open,
their red mouths as they spoke:

'Redwood, private, 7th Reconnaissance.'
'Frank Wight, corporal, 4th Cavalry.'
'Briggs, private, 82nd Airborne.'
'Pete Sherbrook, Brule, Wisconsin.'
'Ruxton, private, 7th Field Artillery.'
'Gibson, John, sergeant, 1st Infantry.'
'Juan Suarez, Arizona.'
'Thompson, Sam, master sergeant, 501st Parachute.'
'Harford Hunt, private first class, 103rd Infantry.'
'Eli Guckenheimer, private, 2nd Marines.'
'Taylor, Edmund, 2nd Battalion, US Rangers.'
'Jay Johnson, Tennessee.'
'Earl Johnson, Alabama.'
'Finch, seaman apprentice, USS *Benham*.'
'Williams, Aaron, Mississippi.'
'Rittenhouse, sergeant, 32nd Infantry.'
'Johnny Red-Bird, El Dorado, Arkansas.'
'George Stagg, private, 36th Armored.'

Their eyes closed again, and there was that sweet smell of rot
in the shifting shadows: a hand
reaching for a bottle; the flare of a struck match
disclosing one man's shoe
split open like a pod,
showing a line of blackened toes.

Off to the side, he caught the bright, avid glance of the coyote
as it turned, limbering away.

★

'So you want to write about the homeless?'
'Yes, sir.'
'Just here, in the city?'
'No, sir. From what I read it's bad all the way up the coast:
San Francisco, Portland, Seattle, Vancouver, eh.
But San Francisco worst of all.'
Overholt got up, stood staring out the window.
'Well, it's something I'd like the paper to address.
It'll make a change from having to hear from Senator McCarthy
about all the Communists spying in the State Department.
I'm happy for you to work on it – putting together a story.
On your own time though, Walker – understand?
We need you on the Desk. Come back to me in a year.'
He looked round then, and smiled. 'Okay: six months.'
He squinted, then, frowning:
'You all right, Walker?
You seem mighty preoccupied for a young fella. Something wrong?'

'I was in a war. I came back, and I'd lost my family.'
'Dead?'
'No. Just lost.'

★

Two years since he arrived at Union Station, and he was back:
needing to see how far he'd come
from the lanterns of Ferguson Alley.
He was sure it was here, and he walked and walked
but there was no alley, no Jerry's Joynt,
and all of Chinatown had gone.
Where there had been streets, stairs and houses,

stores, restaurants, was bare ground,
cleared and graded: a construction site
that one day would become the Hollywood Freeway.
No ginger and cinnamon now, just dust.

★

In the morning, the city appears out of the night's shadow, each building drawing its own darkness under it like a long skirt: head turned to face the first warmth of the sun.

Streets here go on for miles in a straight line, block after block, like stretches of highway, drawn up and parceled out by the maps of real estate and commerce.

I sometimes think about Gitana. Beautiful, of course, but she can't see the depth of anything, just the surface. Going forward with her was hopeless. Like pushing holes in water.

May, 50

★

The new Widmark, *Night and the City*, had just opened
and was showing at the RKO Hillstreet on 8th: a bit out of the way,
but the Golden Gopher was across the street
so he had a couple drinks there and went over. Alone this time.
The credits rolled to hammering bells
and he saw another city he knew
emerging, looming across the water
through nightfall and a scrim of smog:
the Houses of Parliament, Tower Bridge,
Piccadilly Circus all lit up now

94

but the flow of buses and cars
slowed to a fogged dream, filled with sleepwalkers,
streamed ghosts.
Then cut,
to a high-angle shot of a man running,
chased across an open square of shadow and light: this
chessboard of fear, nightmare of traps,
an endless labyrinth of doors and passageways,
and Widmark running, sweating, skittering through a city
turned against him: scrambling over rubble and ruins
to a fatal dawn, and his final descent.
The place he remembered best in London,
but couldn't remember what happened under it:
Hammersmith Bridge.

'The things I did! The things I did!'
'But the wrong things, always the wrong things.'

★

Going down the steps from the Sunshine to Hill Street,
there was a kid's balloon
floating overhead, drifting on
past Royal Liquor on the corner, down
to 3rd and Broad –
a red-brick office-block he'd never noticed before,
right across from the Million Dollar Theater.
More filming, he could tell, with lighting trucks and generators,
rigs and power lines, floods and spots.
It said **BRADBURY**
over the high doorway that he walked straight through.

And he was suddenly inside: there
inside the chest of this giant body – exposed
and displayed, with its balance, its symmetries –
staring up
at this great atrium and the missing hearts
of Los Angeles: two elevators
working up and down in their open cages.

Stairwells, skylights, gantries, balustrades.
The French filigree wrought-iron framework,
the stairs of Belgian marble climbing to the vaulted sky,
all the Mexican floor-tiles, glazed brick, the polished
Californian oak
basking in a hall of light, a hundred feet high.

A miniature city inside a city: intricate,
efficient, and exactly to scale;
perfect in its inner workings, its geometries of light.

Stage machinery, with the grillwork balconies,
roped proscenium, bright acoustic, the light-well drop.

This hidden dream of another century's Europe
here, right here on Broadway; this delirium.
How this city might have been;
or how it *is*, perhaps, if you gaze with the fever of Piranesi
and see the elevators as scaffolds, guillotines
with their cords and pulleys, the toothed wheels
and hanging cables, the block and tackle.
See the deep arches, chains and iron gratings, the high
surveillance walkways, these flights of stairs going nowhere,

streets in the air. A *Carceri d'invenzione*
here in Los Angeles: a limitless maze, prison, theater;
beauty and dread under the bright, unsleeping eye.
The pointless Californian sun.
All hope lost, along with all perspective.

★

Sometimes Los Angeles seems like a series of forts, fenced by free-
ways, heavily policed and lit by flood-light, search-light, torch – and all
watched over by City Hall, the lidless stare of that white panopticon.

June, 50

★

Three men in shirtsleeves stood outside the Bradbury Building:
the tall one, high cheekbones, German-looking, was in charge,
talking to the silent European with the light meter;
next to them, watching, was a big guy with glasses,
sucking in the world like he might explode.
'Bob,' said the director, 'Calm down.'

★

Where the Margaree reaches Lake Ainslie there's a set of pools, shadowed with
trout, stashed with sunlight. We would lie there on the bank, feeling our bodies
healing from the months of cold, swimming in the long pools. I remember the day
I slid in, like a wave through the shallows, low over your shallow form, coming
slow to run aground in you, docking.

On the still lake, that evening, the swan rode out on her reflection like a shield,
sending back slow chevrons to the shore.

★

97

'Shave, mister?'
'Nah, just a trim's fine.'
'You got it!'
Bing Crosby on the radio.
'You live round here, right? Local?'
'Sunshine Apartments.'
'Sunshine in the sunshine, right?'
Walker looked at him in the mirror.
The barber stopped and met his gaze:
'Can't believe we're in a war again.'

★

Cole's was crowded for mid-week. He caught Jimmy's eye:
'Rye, with a short beer chaser.'
'Comin' up, pal.'

Mickey Cohen was in his usual seat in the corner, with a club soda,
glowering at his thugs, the glassy scar under his left eye
flaring sometimes from the neon outside.

'Here you go, friend.'
He took a mouthful of the whiskey and looked around.

'Hand-painted ties, tailored suits, the works.
Not flashy, y'know: *classy* . . .
Bought me these earrings, see?
Peeled off two C-notes for a silver-fox jacket from Bullock's.
He took me out to the Strip last weekend,
dancing at Villa Nova – he says it's better than Ciro's –
and we're highballing along – you follow? – getting friendly

in the back seat of his Cadillac Coupe de Ville
when this rummy stumbles by and chucks up *all* over the hood.
He flips. I mean, he really snaps his cap.
Gets out of the car and goes over to the guy,
pulls out a .45 and blows his freaking face off.
I mean: can you believe that?
You think I should ditch him?'

He took his drinks down the other end of the bar,
settled in there on the corner. 'Pack of Camel plain, Jimmy,'
slipping him a quarter. 'Keep the change.'

'Set her up in the Marmont. Two, three years ago.
When I heard, I drove right over there, you know?
Gave her money for Mexico, choice of doctors.
What more could I do?
Got no ill feelings, in any way *whatsoever*, for that evil bitch.
She was a B-girl when I met her, that broad. Now look at her.
She's got it all.'

There was a stand-off on the way to the can:
'Our boys are going out to die –
being slaughtered in Korea because of traitors like you!'
'How's that again?'
'Saw you writing out names in your little book! Fuckin' Commie!'
Jimmy had her arm by then, leading her out to 6th Street,
'Say – what's the big idea? Get your paws off me!'
The door slammed shut, the conversation
closing over her like water.

★

Out looking for Billy, down on St Julian, he saw a face he knew
sitting out by a dumpster, in a dance of flies.
Velma waved one bandaged hand, tried to get up
but couldn't,
asked his name and waved again.
She looked in her pocketbook; shook it out empty, and stared.
He asked how she was,
and she said her mind had been snowing,
and it made the past so beautiful, now.
Said it was hard, though, to see them:
all the kind faces she used to know,
so many changed or covered over in the fall,
the enormous whiteness, so many just
drifted away.

★

The morning light blades into the room,
and he leans over for a cigarette.
The blinds make planes of sunlight and dust, slices of smoke.
Rita pours herself in through the window, claws
tickering on the linoleum, then stops to watch
a spider, winching itself down from the lampshade.
This is home.

He walked up the Hill, past old folk sitting out in their porches,
up past the Elks Club, the Lovejoy, the Grand,
the pavement still wet from the evening fog
and he went to the little park of benches by the Alta Vista
at 3rd and Bunker Hill Avenue.
He could smell the desert, feel Mojave sand under his feet

from last night's wind.
'Good morning! Beautiful day.'
He looks up at the couple passing, and smiles:
'Sure is. Good morning to you.'

Back down by the Nugent deli, they're filming again.
Same crew: the broad guy with glasses, dark suit, pacing around,
the other two talking. The actor is playing
'The Hall of the Mountain King' on a whistle, very slow
and halting, to a little girl, blond hair in bunches,
holding a balloon on a string,
who laughs and laughs and laughs.

By the Angels Flight Pharmacy
he gets a paper from Red, the one-armed guy.
He watches that fine-looking woman reach out and touch
the 'L' of the Lucky Strike sign
like she does every day.

★

Late September.
Fire season: that hot, dry wind that gets people edgy,
listless, ready to fight but too tired to try, temperatures swinging
and this yellow light from the north
from the smoke of the wildfires burning
up in the tops of the canyons. You can see them at night
like necklaces, tightening.

★

The time Corporal Murray went mad: climbing on top of a trapped German tank, riding on the turret − shouting his head off − waiting for a hatch to open so he could drop in phosphorus or a 36 grenade.

★

The heat was gone. They could feel it.
There was a hectic joy downtown, a release. King Eddy's
six-deep at the bar and still coming.

'Okay, guys. Best killing in the movies.'
'Tommy Udo! It's gotta be Tommy Udo!'
'That's up there, sure, but how about *Raw Deal*
when the broad gets the flambé in the face?'
'Didn't kill her, though.'
'What about *T-Men*,
when The Schemer gets cooked in the steam-room?'
'Nice . . .'
'That other film of his, the Western, what's it called?
Border Incident! That's got a death by *tractor*.'
'Or *Union Station*, half a mile away − death by cattle stampede!'
'I like that shoot-out in the hall of mirrors . . . '
'Nah, too classy. I'd vote for *Decoy* − Jean Gillie
crushing her boyfriend with her car.'
'Yeah, or that chesty dame with the ice-pick, Janis Carter.'
'He survived . . .'
'I'd take Raymond Burr in *Desperate*. Great movie.
The way he goes over the stair-rail at the end
and drops four flights. That's a lulu.'
'Well, if you're talking stairs it's *gotta* be Tommy Udo, *c'mon* . . .'
'Yeah: hard to beat that − tying an old lady to her wheelchair

then pushing her down a flight of stairs.
Widmark's first film, and he was *dynamite*.'
'Okay. All agreed? Right. *Kiss of Death*. Udo gets the cake.'

★

*He remembered the German on the barricade who took a magnesium flare in the
chest and went up like a bonfire: so white you couldn't look, but you couldn't quite
look away.*

★

He dreamt the mountains were on fire
and the flames were gliding down the sides like lava,
the mountains were slipping into the sea which was on fire,
into the city, which was also burning,
and the ground opened up then
and he dreamt that he walked away,
streets full of stones,
and he saw a black man black with flame, black leaves
falling all around him: a black autumn, coming down.
And Pike, he dreamt of Pike,
pinning him by the throat to the ground, with a knife.
And then he woke.

★

There was a new crack through the tiles in the bathroom,
running in a straight line from the window to the door.

★

He was working nights at the *Press*, nights out on the street,
sharpening now after the turn in the year, the air
loosened after the rain, the pavement black and glinting.
There were parts of the city that were pure blocks of darkness,
where light would slip in like a blade to nick it, carve it open:
a thin stiletto, then a spill of white; the diagonal gash
of a shadow, shearing; the jagged angle sliding over itself
to close; the flick-knife of a watchman's torch, the long gasp
of headlights from nowhere, their yawning light – then
just as quickly
their falling away:
closed over, swallowed
by the oiled, engraining, leaden dark.
He hears someone running
but there's no one there.
His shadow folds into the wall, then along it.
Then gone.

★

'Hey, Walker. Wanted in Overholt's office.'

He went through, past the juniors: Pike, talking over
the top of everyone, repeating his punch-line
louder each time, harder.
The old man was checking finals, but he pushed them aside.
'Very well, Walker, you can go this summer. Up to San Francisco.
I like what you've done here on this homeless issue,
so we'll use you as a stringer, see how it goes.
I want a big piece on this, on the whole thing.'
'You mean the destitute?'

'Yes. Out on the streets
while the mayor and the police commissioner
are fine-dining in Chasen's or Musso's Back Room.
I mean the fact that two thirds of this city
is a fenced-off ghetto;
that there's graft and corruption running right the way through.
I mean the fact that this is a country where there aren't enough homes,
enough jobs, where one in six Angelenos are ex-servicemen
and they're lying out on Skid Row –
but all anyone ever talks about is watching for Russians,
HUAC locking up half of Hollywood,
the government building more bombs.
We won the war, but we're living like we lost it.'

He stood, and went to the window.
'Things are hotting up, Walker. It's a good time to go.'

★

Pike just wouldn't stop moving.
Now he was biting his nails: turning his head
to get better purchase,
like he was pulling at a spare-rib
not his own finger, glancing up like Saturn
now and again,
from this useless mess,
his own frayed edge: his only quick.
When he saw Walker he stopped, looked around,
gave the room one of his fascinating smiles.

★

Loch Ban's deep pools and waterways host what light there is, and you can
almost hear the shoots rustling up through the dead leaves left from the fall, the
buds in the trees, their green snapping open.

Father said the same words every spring. 'Let this year bring the luck of milk to
the shielings, the luck of fish to the shores.'

★

He went down to the May Company to find some new clothes:
a sharkskin suit, semi-drape in medium blue,
with two pairs of pants, double-pleated, cuffed.
Some fresh shirts, a better hat, a decent pair of shoes.
Had it all sent over to the Sunshine,
then went to Levy's Grill on Spring
for their one-dollar dinner and a drink.

Thought he'd keep walking afterward, fix this city in his head.
Down Center Place, between Spring and Main
round back of the burlesques and crib-houses,
a girl on the corner, red flower in her hair:
'Hello, sweetheart. You lonesome?
You look lonesome, honey. You want a good time tonight?'
'No. No, thanks.'
All the way north to 1st
and up past the *Times*, and police headquarters,
then west, climbing hard to the Gladden Apartments,
cutting in back
past Olive Court, that weird little neighborhood tucked away,
then rising again
to that space on top of the 2nd Street Tunnel
– on 2nd above Olive

where the streets splay open to the sky –
the Argyle on one side, the Claridge on the other,
the Mission Apartments across from it, and the Dome
way on up there, at the top of the Hill.
Its bright white stucco
and that onion cupola, in terracotta red:
a weathered signpost for the heights of home.

★

There was a message on his desk the next day with a number:
'RING ME,' it said.
The voice was the same, just older.
'How are you, Billy?'
'What say we drop over to Cole's tonight? Or Charlie O's?'
'Sure, but not Cole's, eh . . . Make it Charlie's at eight. That okay?'

It was under the Hotel Alexandria: a crummy dive, but he liked it.
And so did Billy: there in the corner, already started.
He went over, dropping his hat on a hook,
hitching up both pant legs at the knees and sat down,
shaking out a smoke:
'Hey, how you doing, buddy? It's been a year, easy . . .'
'Let's have that drink.' Billy turned to the bar-keep.
'Two ryes. Water on the side.'
'I went looking for you a few times, eh, but no dice.'
'Ah, well. There's a lot to do, y'know. Lot of places to go.
It's only getting worse out there.
The cops getting heavy on the street:
rousting them, tossing their tents, moving them on,
y'know what I mean? Strong-arm stuff. Orders from above.'

'I saw Velma in the summer. She all right?'
'Not so good,' he said, looking down. 'Not so good.
Nobody's in any shape, really. No way to live a life.
You get to be an expert in all sorts down there.
Scabies, scurvy, dermatitis, fungal infections, *bacterial* infections,
Bartonella – that's everywhere – impetigo,
and the bad ones – trench foot, leg ulcers, gangrene.
It's like being back in the war, I tell ya.'
He smiled thinly at his empty glass.
'Same again,' said Walker, tapping the counter, peeling the wrap
off a pack of Old Golds. 'And leave the bottle.'
'You still at the *Press*?'
'Still with them, yeah. Going up the coast for a time . . .
San Francisco.'
It still sounded implausible.
'I'm going to write about this. Skid Row.'
Billy stared at the table. 'Good luck with that.'

'Say, I been meaning to ask – you ever see coyotes on the streets?'
His friend looked up.
'Ah, the Tricksters. Like Reynard, Br'er Rabbit, Anansi.
And fire-bringers, the Indians say. The coyote, and the raven.
They steal fire and bring it to mankind.
You better hope they stay away.'

They went on talking; barely heard the bartender
twisting open a new bottle –
like the sound of a chicken's neck, getting broken.

'And they're closing off the city with these freeways,
saying it *improves connections*,

shutting down sidewalks to *enhance security*.
We're bordered and policed by concrete.
For what? The cult of the car.
To enshrine the *unalienable right* of all Americans to drive one.
To build our lives and cities around them.
But it's worse.
They want us to glide from one enclave to another,
from the apartment building
to the office block in the *Central Business District*
with barely a nod to the security guard.
We're back to circling the wagons.
This is our fear of 'the other'
– Indians, blacks, Mexicans, Communists, *Muslims*, whatever –
America has to have its monsters,
so we can zone them, segregate them,
if possible, shoot them.
They call this *patriotism, Nativism*,
but it's racialism, pure and simple. And paranoia.
Now that America's gone abroad, to fight a war – *two* wars –
we're frightened, frightened that foreigners
might come over here and do the same to us.'

He stopped then, and there was a grim smile.
'Bugsy Siegel, Police Chief William Parker, Mickey Cohen,
Richard Nixon, Jack Dragna, Senator Joseph McCarthy . . .
Jesus. Christ. Almighty.'
He looked up at the ceiling.
Laughed out loud:
'It's like someone shook the map of America
and all the crap that wasn't bolted down
ended up here, in Los Angeles.'

He stopped again, and his eyes shifted.
'I don't know if it's three years, five years, ten,
but I'm telling you, friend, this city's getting ready to blow.'

★

That night, in buying stuff at Budget Basket, there was a tremor:
shoppers down on their hands and knees in the middle of the aisle,
looking up at the shelves, shaking,
cans rattling, all by themselves,
beer bottles, rolling backward and forward on the floor.

★

That night he heard a door open, and footsteps on the tiles around the
pool, and the clink of ice in a glass on the table next to him.
But there was no drink, no pool, no door, and no outside, no other's
footsteps than his own as he crossed the room to check it was a dream.
The night was black through the window. On the dead rails of Angels
Flight: the coyote's eyes were lit like miners' lamps.

1951

A dream of wild-fires, earthquake, tidal waves.

He wakes and opens his eyes.
The city is there, stretching to the white horizon.

He blinks, and the city is gone.

★

Daybreak on the 101: mountains on the right,
the Catalinas far behind, and the Channel Islands – Santa Cruz
and Santa Rosa – gleaming like flakes of coal in the new sun.

As the highway straightened north, away from the ocean,
the view thinned down
to chicken-dinner shacks, roadhouses, motels,
the oil fields of Santa Maria.

The colossal woman in the seat across
watches her daughter
running up and down the aisle of the bus –
glares narrowly at her
over a root beer and a giant sack of funnel cake.

115

Snapping, at last: 'SPATULA!' she blares.
'I got two words for you. *Be-have.*'

After four hours of this,
when he finally saw the ocean again at Pismo Beach,
he knew he'd had enough:
when they pulled in for a rest-stop at San Luis Obispo
he took his bag and got out,
made his way to the turn for Highway 1.

★

'Don't normally pick up hitch-hikers, but you're a soldier, right?'
He was looking at the duffle bag.
'I was, yeah. How far you heading?'
'Frisco.'
'Same here, eh. Thanks.'

The coastal fog like battle-smoke, but burning off
as they drove north, through the morning,
ocean on one side
and the black slopes of the canyons on the other, showered
with the arrow-falls of pale white pampas grass.

'Name's Ed. Ed Newell.'
'Walker.'
'I need to take a break. Get some coffee.'

They pulled in at a rest-stop with a beat-up shack
and the ocean below, and a steep path to the beach.
The fog had cleared from the heads of the redwoods
and he could see enormous birds

116

hanging in the thermals above the trees.
'Condors,' Ed told him, 'Ten-foot wingspan.
And look. You ever seen the Statue of Liberty?'
'Yeah.'
Ed nodded to the redwoods: 'Them trees grow taller.'
They took their sandwiches and coffee down;
sat on the rocks by the sea.
The beach was strewn with huge green cables of kelp
alive with beach hoppers, rove beetles, roly-polies
– what they called *slaters* back home.
Beyond that, an outcrop of boulders that suddenly shifted
and there was a snuffling, snoring sound
as a great stone rose up on the back of another
with a grunt and a low growling. A roar.
When you made out one, you saw them all:
beasts the size of automobiles – elephant seals.
'They're molting, look.'
Walker saw that their fur was trailing in ribbons
like the torn clothes of the men out on the street.
'I've seen a lot of seals,' he said, 'But nothing like this.
They must be twenty feet long.'
'I do this trip every week,' Ed said.
'Always try to stop on this headland.
Last time I saw sea-otters out there,' he said, grinning,
'lying on their backs eating abalone.'
'What line of business you in?'
'Oh, y'know. Sales. But I like looking at things, y'see?'
'Yeah,' Walker smiled. 'I see.'

Half an hour down the road, around Point Sur,
he pulled in hard to the shoulder, and threw open his door.

'Blue whales!' he shouted, 'A pair of them . . .'
They just stood there, then, at the cliff-edge,
staring so hard their eyes teared up.
Standing together, wiping their eyes and laughing.

★

*The smell of the sea; the larks rising in the wind over Dunvegan, tiny banners
broken open. The sound of the stream's fast-running water, on through the high
wood. Her soft eyes, her mouth. Those days under the lenient trees, as I lay in the
shielings with Annie MacLeod.*

★

'Hey, Walker.'
'Hmn?'
'It's Monterey. You want to get some proper food?'

He parked the Mercury right by the harbor,
and they walked down to the wharf and its forest of masts.
The nets were out drying, getting mended,
the decks hosed down, some men already taking a drink.
There were a few places open, though it was barely six.
'This one's on me, by the way,' said Walker,
seeing a place on the corner, Tarantino's Seafood.
'How about here?'
'Nah. There's a real one farther down. Authentic.'
The Liberty looked the same as all the others:
checked table-cloths faded by the sun, tin ashtrays, battered chairs.
They had a plate of oysters, grilled sardines,

clam chowder in sourdough bowls.
'How's that?' said Ed, wiping his mouth.
'Tastes like home.'
'What time you got?'
'Twenty of seven.'
'We better get on the road. Keep the light.'

★

They hit the city by nine, with the neon coming on.
'This is Union Square,' he said, 'and here's my hotel.'
It was like the Biltmore, only smaller, and just one doorman.
'Welcome to the St Francis, sir.'
'Sorry I can't take you on, Walker. I'm pretty bushed.
It's North Beach, right? You can get a cab here.'
'Nah, I'll walk. Thanks, eh – thanks for everything.'
'No problem. Two blocks that way, then left on Grant.
Keep walking till you reach the top. Adios!'

He had an address from Overholt, some alley off Grant,
above Union, it said, so he started north in a straight line
through a Chinatown that seemed familiar,
feeling the land rise under his feet and the air clearing
till he felt himself climbing, like he was
on the 3rd Street steps again,
rising above the city and its lights.
He recognized the white tower, lit up above him
on the top of the hill, then gone from sight,
and next thing he was there, at the right address:
ringing the doorbell, and the house super giving him his key
and pointing: 'Top of the stairs.'

119

The room was small – a Murphy bed, a table and a chair –
but the view made up for it:
the last red stains of sunset and the bright, rolling lights
of the city streets like a fairground underneath.
He pulled out the pint he'd been saving
and raised it to the window: 'To San Francisco,'
he heard himself say: putting the bottle's
open mouth to his, and drinking.

★

*I turned to her in the night, again and again, in some dream, stiffening against
her, shined her through and through.*

*Lying there afterwards, completed, emptied out, staring at the ceiling hand in
hand.*

Her clear blue eyes.

★

He found himself misplaced in his bed all night, mislaid.
His watch said morning, but the window's light was milky,
like gauze on the lens,
and there was nothing to see but fog,
the occasional rooftop, tree or church spire
dipping in and out of sight.
He took a shower, dressed, looked again.
There was a hole in the weather
he watched the sun smoke through.

He was near the top of Telegraph Hill, so he climbed Coit Tower,
saw the last scarves of fog still caught in the valleys,
in the deep slots of narrow streets, in the ficus trees,
and the city was slowly unwrapping itself
in its gray and gold, with its bridges – lit, dazzling, high-
wired across the blue panoply of the bay
and its yachts, the far headlands, the scuttled ship of Alcatraz.

It was like living in a dune of Bunker Hills,
with proper weather and a better view;
the switchback streets like the rides on Coney Island,
the bay as bright as the Gulf of St Lawrence.

★

A postcard of the Golden Gate Bridge, to Annie MacLeod, Dunvegan, Inverness County, Cape Breton, Nova Scotia, Canada

Dear Annie, I told you I would reach the other side and here I am! Not much to report. I have a good job on a newspaper in Los Angeles and they've sent me up here for a spell. Weather changeable – just like home, which is good! But much warmer: 70°! I should have written before, but it's all been so new. Such a change. I hope you are well, and keeping up with your piano lessons. I think of you often, mostly of the times by Lake Ainslie or up in the meadows that summer, before all this. Before the war. We were so happy. I want to be happy again.

Please give my regards to your mother and father.

July, 51

★

He walked it, easy, those first weeks: the produce market
down at Washington and Davis,
the ferries and wharfs of the Embarcadero;
the hidden gardens of Telegraph Hill; the Presidio, the park.
He remembered, now, how he knew that hotel in Union Square,
Edmond O'Brien stayed there in *D.O.A.*,
and why he recognized that bar in Chinatown, Li Po, because
Orson Welles is chased past its door in *The Lady from Shanghai*.
Months later, he finds Bacall's apartment in *Dark Passage*,
high on Montgomery, by the Filbert Steps,
guarded by hawthorn and dragon trees.

★

The sun wobbles in the water of the bay: lattices of light.
The nets of sunlight in the water, the same nets as home.
August, 51

★

He got to work. From the heights to the depths: Howard Street,
south of Market, between 3rd and 4th,
a few blocks away from the *Chronicle*.
He found a Salvation Army troupe with tambourines
singing in a semi-circle round a bunch of bums: men oblivious
to everything but their jugs of wine.
There's deep discussion, laughing, hugging,
then a shower of loose punches, and the Army scattering,
some solemn gulps of wine
then more laughs, back-slapping, fumbled rolling of cigarettes.

122

Everyone wanted to be somewhere else:
the Chicago Café, the New York Hotel, the Mars Hotel.
They panhandled from 3rd to 6th, Tehama to Minna,
bought their booze at Pete's Place – 40¢ a jug –
slept it off in a cot in a flophouse for pretty much the same.

There was a guy on his own, in his forties maybe:
no socks; cuffs and collar black with grime, hands
empty and shaking; famished eyes.
On his lapel, a Silver Star.

'How you doing, buddy?'
'Could use a little lush.'
'You serve in the war?'
'Yeah. Fought all over, then came back to nothing.
My girl gone. Job gone. Got played for a chump.'
He poured the last three fingers from a fifth of white port.
'How old are you?'
'I dunno. What year is it?' He gave a flat laugh. 'Who cares.
I was born in '20.'
'Same year as me, friend.'
He lowered his eyes like an animal does, losing the fight.
Walker closed two dollars in the soldier's hand, shook it and left.

★

He learned the city was a place of pockets.
The Row was small and barely spilled; two blocks either side
and you wouldn't even know it was there.
It was the same with the weather. Constantly changing
but always local. You went east round a hill
and it rose ten degrees.

The west had a different climate, kept its haar, its sea mists –
it was where the winds came from.
He took a streetcar to Point Lobos
to see it, the edge of the ocean, Cliff House,
looking out over Seal Rocks, the fog
rolling in like smoke.
There was that end-of-season melancholy about the rest:
the pleasure palaces of the Sutro Baths,
with its neon sign reading 'Tropic Beach',
and the amusement park, which he wandered through,
with the wind chasing paper wrappers round in circles –
Playland-at-the-Beach where Welles
came to, in the Crazy House,
and blew out the mirrors, walking away
past Laff in the Dark and Shoot the Chutes
and leaving it all behind, heading for the gray Pacific,
in *The Lady from Shanghai.*

★

*The fishermen with the long stares would say the haar is the sea's breath, and the
sea over shingle a dying man's rattle. It was true for Lachlan from Pleasant Bay,
with his face full of shrapnel and the death-shudders. I spaded his pack in after his
remains; we were under fire, so a foot-deep had to do.*

★

On the way to his diner on Columbus
or one of his bars, La Rocca's, Tony Nik's or the Northstar,
he passed Washington Square.
The winos are there: sprawled around

all day with their paper bags,
before some outrage sets them squabbling like gulls.

★

Do they notice the air has sharpened, that the trees are letting go the
last of themselves, the maple's red dress already spilled to the ground?

The trees in fall like my father: dying from the head down.

October, 51

★

She was sitting up at the counter in an empty bar that afternoon.
The hydrangea-pink and mauve of her flowery hat
picked out the redness in her eyes,
those thread-veins round her nose.
She was talking to herself, or to the whiskey glass,
it was hard to tell, but she was in the middle of something:
'He was getting fresh, putting the make on me,
shooting me some line about being a Hollywood hot dog,
getting kick-backs from the Mob or something.
I said, You know what? Are you fucking kidding me?
Give me a break. And he says, C'mon, don't be a sap,
I'm on the square, sweetheart, honest to God!'
She paused, and took a mouthful, then looked over at him.
'Buy me a drink?'
He nodded to the barman. 'Leave the bottle.'
'Say, that's mighty generous. You're okay, fella.
You're an okay guy in my book!'
He joined her at the bar, studying her closely.

125

She was picking at a darn in the elbow of her cardigan,
scratching an itch, readjusting her position on the stool,
eyes fixed on the one still point: her glass.
He could almost see where she lost her way.
It's the first crease in the leather, a fold in paper,
the way the smile or frown goes
and the shape is made, the direction taken.
She was pretty bombed already; started singing
a verse of a song, then forgot it.
She looked like she'd been drunk for years;
a piece of metal
that's been worked so often it's lost its give.
Next time someone tried to bend her, she'd just snap.
'I'll remember you,' she said with a sloping grin.
'Lady, you'll remember me till the bottle's gone.
And don't forget what they say:
there's a message in every one of these bottles.
But you can't read it till you got it empty.'

★

*Cadent rain through paper birch, the days sliding through each other; the search
for some way to make a mark, some kind of legible life.*

★

There's a film-crew outside The Paper Doll on Union,
and a framed poster *At the Piano – Jean Darr*
but it's Marie Windsor in the photograph,
and there's a bullet-hole in the glass.

A few days after, they've sealed off Filbert Street at Grant,
and cops with megaphones are keeping back crowds
at the auto repair shop on the corner.
He knows the director from a mugshot in the papers:
Dmytryk, one of the Hollywood Ten,
back in business after naming names.

On the cover of *Time* magazine a week later: Senator Joe McCarthy.

★

He heads downtown on a Saturday night, the cable-cars
clanging through the streets. Long after they've gone
you can still hear those cables, rattling underground.
At the Powell Street turnaround outside the Owl Drug Company
he walks west for the Tenderloin, to hear Dave Brubeck
live at the Black Hawk: to watch
Chet Baker watching Paul Desmond
on alto, gliding through 'Stardust', 'You Go to my Head'.

★

He strolls the Barbary Coast at night, or where it once was,
down on Pacific and Montgomery,
now known as the 'International Settlement',
where the military shore patrols in their overcoats and gloves
pair up with regular cops
and watch their boys don't get into trouble
in the sex-clubs or queer bars or brothels.

One time he saw two men bust out of a crib-joint, naked,
both with knives, it looked like: one black,

one white – though it was pretty hard to tell as they jabbed
and parried under Margie's sputtering bulb –
and over real quick:
one slash opened the black guy's buttock
like a plum, then this neat stab to the throat
and with it
a twisting rope
so hot it steamed
as it splashed on the cobbles;
the blood that ran out of him
till he ran out of blood.
It could have been any of us, he supposed,
weltering in our own muck,
all bled out in that back alley
three thousand miles from home.

★

I was talking to this North Shore corporal and I'd just looked round to check the
road and turned back and he wasn't there. He was down in the culvert. Sniper
got him in the middle of his forehead. The back of his head was gone, brains and
everything, gone.

★

He thought about Billy, all those men on the street in Los Angeles.
About Overholt. Even Sherwood and Rennert.
He tried to remember the Mexican girl,
how all she wanted was a house in Bel Air –
to go to Hollywood parties, watch television, and gossip,
but he couldn't gather her together in his head.

It snagged at him every time he thought about her,
the way of a rag-nail in a pocket's silk lining.
Strange that:
his memory full of holes, hers always tight as a fist.

★

He loved having weather again,
the way it changed every minute.
They closed the Golden Gate in December, for a tempest
wrecking boats on Ocean Beach,
and the next month there was snow.

★

He'd been given some name by Overholt: a guy in UC Berkeley
he should talk to, Walter Friedländer in Social Welfare,
so he made the call after Christmas,
took the Key train over the bay through banks of fog
so dense he couldn't see the water.

'Please sit down, Mr Walker. You look tired.' The tall man
with clever eyes and a slight German accent
would meet him many times that year, preferring lunch
at Spenger's Fish Grotto down by the marina –
for the clear light, as much as the shellfish, he said,
'You can see San Quentin from here . . .'

A Social Democrat and Jew, who'd lived through Weimar,
got out of Berlin in '33, knew his history of displacement, tyranny.
They talked about all the émigré directors and cinematographers,

writers and actors, and the old man laughed: 'At last!
German Expressionism meets the American Dream!'

He'd worked with the homeless, with ex-soldiers,
all through the west coast,
said it would get worse when the Republicans won that year,
which they would, he knew,
that he was frightened for the first time here in America:
'McCarthyism is fascism. Exactly the same. Propaganda and lies,
opening divisions, fueling fear, paranoia. Just like the thirties:
a state of emergency, followed by fascism, followed by war.
You've just defeated Hitler.
Can't anyone see you've made another, all of your own?'

The last time they met, walking round the marina after lunch,
he said his worry now was the streets would get worse –
whatever happened in the election – because of mental-health reform.
'They're calling it *deinstitutionalization*,
– which is a hard word for me to say! –
and the theory is good: close down asylums,
which are medieval, dirty, corrupt and over-crowded,
and give community care with cheaper drugs.
In practice, though, this is all about money. As usual.
The sick will miss their medication and – how do you say it? –
fall through the cracks. They will be homeless,
ending up in prisons or out on the streets.
There will be thousands of them.
This is the future, my friend. This is the future.'

★

He sees the Dmytryk movie, *The Sniper*. All filmed round here.
It could have been him at the end, running uphill,
running to ground: Filbert between Battery and Sansome,
the Lower Filbert Steps, Vallejo at Montgomery,
then up from Union through Varennes to his place, finally,
an upstairs room at 450 Filbert Street, east of Grant,
where the cops find him sitting with his rifle, crying.

★

The view from the window was west, over to Russian Hill,
and the bay, and the Golden Gate.
He doesn't deserve this city,
its play of height and depth, this
changing sift of color and weather.
The water held in it a shimmy of light
and the days were warming through June and July
and the road that threads through the hem of the Highlands
would now be decked with wild stock, lupins and apple blossom
all the way to Chéticamp and Pleasant Bay.
She will be wearing her sleeveless dress, cornflower blue
and walking away.
He could not call her back to his life: which is a horror,
which is the dead calf in the bank-head field, a black flap
bubbling with maggots,
ugly and wrong.
Her clean eyes could not see this,
what he has become.

★

A postcard of Telegraph Hill, to Annie MacLeod, Dunvegan, Inverness County, Cape Breton, Nova Scotia, Canada

Dear Annie, you would like San Francisco I think. It's very dramatic with all these houses scrambling up over the hills, and the bay and the bridges and everything, but you might not care so much for the crowds. You've never seen so many people! It's not like New York or Los Angeles, mind. Halifax seems like a village to me now.

Do you ever think of those days, those summers?

My best regards to your parents, and all those that remember me.

August, 52

★

Summer was closing, and he moved through the last of it,
finding a park with fairground music
coming from somewhere behind the trees.
Walking round, he understood that the funfair
is nothing to do with cork-shoots or coconut shies,
the carousel, the booster or the bumper rides,
not balloons-and-darts, not the cotton-candy,
ice-cream, salt water taffy or fries – it's fear,
it's the high-wheel of fortune and despair: that
thin glimpse of joy and freedom, before
rattling back to earth, loose-legged and spinning.

The real carnival is the other side –
beyond the midway, the concession stands, 'Hot dogs
a nickel, three for a dime', the merry-go-round

with its lights and bobbing horses, the churning calliope,
shouts, screams, sprays of laughter, gimcracks, baubles,
stuffed animals, those feather-headed
Kewpie dolls on sticks,
the children crying out, the barkers calling.
Follow the lights:
the colored electric bulbs strung up
on spitting wires, the smell of burning fat and engine oil,
cheap perfume, sweat and food and dung.
Here are the pinheads, the half-boys, the lobster-boys,
snake-men, midgets; the cage
and the geek inside, the man with the horrors,
waiting to eat the heads off chickens
for a bed of wet straw and a pint of rye.

This is not the worst.
The worst is the hall of mirrors
where you catch sight of yourself, twisted,
swollen, unrecognizable.
Then a beautiful woman – your wife, your lover.
Then it's you again: old, crippled;
her as a turning witch, you as the held man.
And you blow every piece of your glass apart.
It's the worst thing in the world,
catching sight of yourself.

The next day, the carnival is gone.
All that's left is the flattened grass
and trodden ground,
the litter of popcorn boxes,
Dixie cups and empty bottles.

It looks like the place
where some huge, fantastic beast had foraged
and lain for a while
before moving on.

★

All the tourist films call California a playground, solely designed for our
entertainment – colorful, exotic, transporting, like a carnival – and it *is*
just that: a carnival. A crude travesty of childhood happiness: a pageant
of loss.

I feel closer to her here, with the water all around. The light.

Annie.

Torn apart, the length of our lives.

September, 52

★

There was a ticker-tape parade in town for Eisenhower:
A hundred thousand, the papers said,
the headlines: WE LIKE IKE.
A month later he was in, on a landslide,
soldier on a soldier's ticket: get us out of Korea;
get the Communists out of here, and everywhere else.

★

The view from the window was gray, tumbling. The fog,
breaking in waves from the west,

had already taken Russian Hill
and only the towers of the Golden Gate Bridge still stood
above the layer of mist, pouring
its dry ice into every crack of the city.
The occasional sunbeams like search-lights; the two-tone
moan of the foghorn blowing.
Our boys laid smoke so you could hardly see the beach
and the black dots. Some of them moving;
most of them not.
A sudden blazing, like gas flares from an oil-well, but lateral –
the flame-thrower tanks
burning off the sides of the beach – and you could hear nothing
but the drumfire that beat in our faces,
shivered our ungrounded souls.
Only the sea opened its arms to us.
Welcoming, drinking us down.

★

*The waters of Loch Ban steam in the white dusk. The pines creak under fresh
snow, and squirrels watch as I pass, each holding on to the base of their tree. The
gull-like screech of the bald eagles, high in a stand of balsam fir, their blood-call
over the wastes where the trout or the rabbit feel the closing claws: their drawing-
up and their down-fall.*

★

When he was working with the derelicts downtown
he'd taken to using the Hotel Utah,
a few blocks south of Howard.
Today was quiet, just a few in, and the owner,

who sat in the same corner each day,
staring out, on guard,
until you got real close
and saw his trick, how he'd had eyes
tattooed on his lids – that he was
asleep, or out cold. Like those
French façades with the shutters spread,
not windows at all
just paint on a stuccoed wall.
Eyes shut, tight as clams,
saliva pooling on his vest.

'Howdya like that guy?'
Some boozehound he'd never seen in before,
holding grimly onto the counter like it was the gunwale of a boat.
His mouth moved a bit before he came up with:
'Hey, Mac. Talkin' to you.'
'He's the head honcho round here, so don't make a book of it.'
A couple in the corner were taking notice. The man strolls over.
'You're outta line, bud. Take a walk,
or you'll be wearing your asshole like a collar.'
The drunk swings round, eyes loosening:
'You can take your lousy bar an' shove it, fuckin' . . .'
The guy knocked him down, and out,
then bent over
and hit him again: a savage one-two to the face.
The way his girl looked at him then.
Like she'd let him do *anything*.

★

The fighting over in Korea, and our boys were coming home;
just as he was finishing all this
in San Francisco and going back to what felt like war.
He went down to Fisherman's Wharf for a last meal,
past the steaming kettles of the crab-stands,
all the restaurants, Alioto's, DiMaggio's, Sabella and La Torre,
but just wasn't hungry, and kept walking,
stopping at Speedy's up on Union and Montgomery
for a sandwich and a bottle
and went back, and sat at the window.

★

I was walking in the high country, among the cave-systems, when I found it: that bone knife laid down in the sixth century and picked up again in this.

American cities have no past, no history. Sometimes I think the only American history is on film.

August, 53

★

The echo of running feet still loud on the waterfront,
down the Montgomery Steps, and all through Chinatown.
Rita Hayworth is still driving up Sacramento
past the Brocklebank; the sniper
still crying in that upstairs room on Filbert Street;
Agnes Moorehead still falling
from her window at the Tamalpais, and Bogart
– always running – still scrabbling down its fire-escape.

137

Joan Crawford leaves by the door of that building,
still chased in one sequence
from Greenwich and Hyde in San Francisco
to Cinnabar Street, three blocks from the Sunshine – flickering
from Russian Hill to Bunker Hill in twenty-four frames.
Jack Palance, trying to drive into her
down 2nd to Olive by the Mission Apartments,
only seeing in the last moment
it's really Gloria Grahame, his lover –
crashing, and killing her, and himself,
at the dead-end parapet above the 2nd Street Tunnel.

The street he'll be walking, in under a week.

★

He dreamt a plane carrying troops crash-landed
onto the cemetery outside Caen, and the long-dead
were churned up with the newly-dead
and he had to walk through it all.
Looking for himself.

★

The view from the window is black,
with a hundred moving lights – red, green and white –
the way he always dreamed the flight-deck of a plane.
Another sunset bloods the bay
back into slaughter, back to
bodies on the barbed-wire
– the larder of the butcher-bird –
back to taking that house in Villons,

138

grappling with the German.
Feeling the panic
triggering at the other's neck, the pump
of the rounds going into him,
underneath you – the jolts – and he was reaching
in between you for your Browning
and you could smell his skin burning on it,
they get so hot, the barrels.
Till you emptied the magazine;
pulled away wet, and spent.

That dream of the mess hall, cavernous in shadow,
full of all the fallen,
line after line of the regiment's dead, who raise their eyes to you,
the living betrayer, then lower their heads.

1953

Looking down through the night on the way to Los Angeles
he heard this noise over his tinnitus,
over the plane's engines: a screaming.
The stewardess was standing over him – frightened,
it looked like.
Someone in his seat was screaming.

Seen from above,
the city was a network of hot, red wires
like a grill;
a geometry of grid and parallel lines
all the way to a vanishing point.
The headlights on the freeway
a lava thread through the Hollywood hills.

'She's a real beauty, ain't she?' The guy across from him had said,
nodding at the view. They'd passed over downtown –
City Hall, like a white crucifix
up-ended in the ground –
but there was a giant tangle of freeway
knotted up north of there, lit up like Christmas,
and that's what he meant. 'The Four Level Interchange.
Makes you proud to be an American.'

'You live downtown?'
'Hell, no. Me and my family, we got a nice place in Orange County:
Yorba Linda, home of Richard Nixon. Decent white town.'

★

It was like watching a ciné-film from the future:
things familiar but wrong.
He noticed the yellow smog, thin and bitter; desert grit in the air.
Going up the 3rd Street steps the palms were even blacker
from the traffic going through the tunnel,
the paintwork on the windows of the Belmont
more cracked than ever.
The Sunshine a little shabbier: older, just like him,
but pretty much the same.
The desk-clerk didn't recognize him at first,
then grinned: 'You want your old room back? It's just come free.
Pretty much most of them are free, now I think of it.'

He took a walk up the Hill, dropped some shoes off at Varney's
to get re-heeled, some shirts next door at Mr Yee's.
Got a haircut at the barbers next to the pharmacy.
'Shave, mister?'
'Yeah, why not.'
'You got it!'
Bing Crosby on the radio.

★

The *Press* the next morning, and it hadn't changed: the clatter
of Teletype and typewriters, the calls of '*Copy!*'
He was due to see Overholt first thing, in his office.

146

'I like what you've done, Walker. Interesting stuff.
I want you to bring yourself up to date with how it is here,
on the street, then we'll run the whole story over a couple weeks.'
He looked up from his sheaf of papers:
'Oh, by the way, I promoted Pike.
He's joining you on the City Desk.'

He caught up with Sherwood and Rennert in their bar on 2nd,
and the end of one of Rennert's speeches:
'I mean . . . dinner, a bottle, a bed an' a girl – that too much to ask?'
blowing a long stream of smoke at the ceiling.
'Ah, Mr Walker! Back from the boondocks! Welcome.'
'Thanks. So, what's the dope?'
'Well, the bad news is that we've gotten real busy.
There're a lot more people in this city and a lot more getting killed.
When you were here – '50, '51 – it was mostly strong-arm stuff,
muscle jobs, knives occasionally. Right? Now it's shooters.
The Mob's into everything, including the cops.'
'And the good news?'
'There ain't any. Except Overholt's still got all his buttons.'
'And Pike?'
'He's got his eyes open.'
'For buttons?'
'Lighten up, Walker. Have a smoke.' Sherwood dug in his pocket,
threw a pack of Kents across the table. 'They're new. Filtered.'
'No thanks,' he said, 'I'll stick to what I know.'

★

He went looking for Billy every evening, five nights straight;
found him on the Friday, in Craby Joe's of all places,

the whole room getting a load on, heeling and toeing:
fat guys cupping peanuts into their mouths, cheering home runs,
pointing at the television with their bottles of Schlitz.
He pushed through to him, and there was a woman
hanging on his arm, swaying.
Her ragged smile, like her slip was showing,
made him look away.
'Hey, Canada!'
'Hello, Billy. How you doing?'
'Good, *good*. This is Ruby.'
'It's *Pearl*,' she said bluntly.
'We gotta go, Pearl – sorry. Business.'

They went out the back, down Center Place, the alley,
now called Harlem Place, apparently, down 6th to Main,
and he was juiced-up and jumpy, wanting to try everywhere.
They checked in at the Gayety, where he knew the doorman –
sat next to a weedy guy watching the burlesque girls: rapt,
biting on a napkin for comfort
– then left, after ten minutes, for some new Mexican bar.
Walking between 5th and 3rd, the Muse had closed,
the Follies and the Jade were still there, but the Regal was gone;
just a gap in the street like a tooth had been pulled.

'So, you see how it's changing?'
'I saw that freeway stack coming in on the plane. They finally did it.'
'No one to stop them. That's almost the end of public transport;
now they're killing public housing. You hear about that?'
'Police Chief Parker?'
'Yeah. Anything Senator McCarthy can do . . .
So Parker fingers the Housing Authority as a bunch of Commies,

public housing as "creeping socialism", and now – wait for it –
community development is shelved for *corporate* development.
Much more important.
And, courtesy of Mr Chandler's *Los Angeles Times*,
he's got a Republican mayor on his side, Norris Poulson,
and they're going after Chavez Ravine.'
'How do you mean? That's allocated for housing, eh?'
'At the moment. But they've cleared it – most of it –
all those Mexican farmers, growing their own food on that land
the last hundred years. Once it's cleared, that's it.
The CRA can do anything.
We're only doing our jobs, they keep saying.
Seems like lying's just part of that job.'
He stopped, and rubbed his eyes.
'More drink, my friend. I'm getting thirsty!'

They talked about San Francisco, about Skid Row, there and here,
then from nowhere he said: 'You had a girl back home,
in Nova Scotia. You gonna see her again?'
Walker took a long pull on his bottle,
tapped out another cigarette, lit it,
drew in deeply; blew. 'I can't, Billy.
The island. My family. Annie. It's all gone now.'
He stared hard at the floor.
'I can't let her see me. What I've become.'

★

He'd stumbled out of there, blurred from drink
like an accidental photograph,
through the fog pinked by the neon lights,

149

bumping his way
against walls and doors up 3rd
to Angels Flight, still open.
He put a penny down, carefully, on the metal tray
and the ticket-man looked at him:
'Don't you know, son? It's a nickel now.'

★

As he lay in bed, he saw that
trying to forget was the same as trying to remember.
A lifetime's work, and damn near impossible.
He pulled out a smoke,
swallowed what was left in the heel of a bottle.
In Cape Breton there was just the past.
Here in California, they're only thinking about the future –
the past is being torn down every day,
so there's no past here to remember.
He stubbed out his cigarette, lay back down in the dark.

★

He wakes to the chatter of a bluejay,
the squeaking cables of the rail-cars, sunlight
levering in through the blinds.

The crack in the wall becomes a lizard.
The corpse in the chair resolves itself
into a pile of clothes and a hat.
The spider comes out of the cornice:
turns the fly round and round,
swathes and wraps it

150

till it looks like a gray bottle,
then drinks it down.
In the bathroom he sees the corpse, now standing,
puts his hand under the running faucet
and recoils,
not knowing if the burn is freeze or scald.

★

He followed the old folk down the steps to town, stopping
as they stop: to catch their breath, pause and check their pockets,
blow their noses, exchange a greeting; men elaborately
raising their hats to the ladies, wishing them 'Good day'.
He stood with them on the corner, by the liquor store,
unsure when to cross, then
stepping off the curb just as the lights change, and the cars
jump forward and stop with a lurch, horns going,
and they all clamber back up, feeling for the lamppost,
holding on to the stop-sign.

He stands looking into the window of the Giant Penny store
on Hill Street, the five-and-dimes, the army-navy stores,
and all around him are pensioners shuffling past, drawn down
by the heat of the sun out of their apartments up on the Hill.
He walks on, south, thinking he might go to the square,
or the library, or a café – Clifton's or Schaber's –
that the air's doing him good,
just the moving about, getting the blood going somewhere.

Pershing Square was a building site, stripped clean.
'Hey, Pop – what gives? Where're all the trees?'

'Dug 'em all up to make way for underground parking.
It's the new thing. Seems pretty cock-eyed to me.
Shipped all them palms and bamboos to Disneyland, they say,
for the Jungle Cruise ride, whatever that is.
No place to sit out now – read the papers, meet neighbors, talk.
No place for us older folk. Just to take a walk down here,
watch things going on . . . Just to sit, you know?'

On the corner of 5th and Broad, there was a guy shouting,
eyes white in his head, hands waving, spittle flying,
something about trumpets, the house of the Lord:
'. . . You have transgressed my covenant, trespassed against my law.
You have set up kings, but not by me. From your silver and gold
your workmen made idols, but this is not God.
The calf of Samaria shall be broken in pieces.
For you have sown the wind. You have SOWN THE WIND . . .'

★

I catch my reflection one night in a Packard's front wing, under the
spike of a streetlight. See a dead man; crosses for eyes.

The tick tack of footsteps down a side-street, disappearing.

November, 53

★

Pike, the pistol, never far away, and never still, as if
he had to keep moving
or the blood might not reach the end of those long extremities.
He was there at the water-cooler, dropping names,

talking over people, pushing into the frame,
waiting for the moment to smile.
In his state of self-enchantment, he'd had a button printed:
I'M A REPORTER AT THE PRESS.
There he was again,
clicking his ballpoint pen down the corridors,
checking himself in the glass of every door.
He was stalking like a stray dog
hungry through the city streets, restless, learning the short cuts,
eating anything.
One of *us*, now, but still rising, unsatisfied, insolent
to all but the boss – for the time being at least:
poor old Overholt, who thinks
this is the son he never had,
the smart young reporter *he* once was
– all those years ago –
thinks *this is the future.*
Pike gazes at Overholt,
attentively; examining
the slowing pulse at the old man's throat.

Walker didn't know why he started to follow Pike that day,
but he did.

★

There was a chill in the fog
that smoked round the lights of the downtown stores
bright with their tinsel and trees,
the signs in the market for **TURKEYS 39¢**,
the day-old-bread counter busy with pensioners

153

testing each loaf or inspecting their change.
Pike pushed past them,
clicking his fingers impatiently – *snap, snap, snap* –
then lifting an apple from the top of a pile
and striding off, biting four chunks from it
then throwing it away.

He watched him check the vending-machines and phone-slots
for nickels or dimes, like that's his job, that he's in charge of that,
squinting at Korean 10-hwan coins
and dropping them noisily in the tips tray at the sandwich bar,
palming two quarters in return –
which he used to buy *Playboy* magazine, the first issue,
Marilyn Monroe on the front, rolling it up,
quick as a shot, and making for the john.

★

In the bar on 2nd, he could see Sherwood and Rennert
busy over a bottle in one of the stalls, talking
loud enough to hear:
'You can't get an angle on Walker, y'know?
He's a tricky bastard – not easy at all.
Like trying to catch a dropped knife.'
'Yeah – you're on the nose there, buddy.'
'And you know what?
Ain't nothing lucky you can do with a knife.'

★

Rennert was right about knives.
The Kraut in Nijmegen he ran

with his bayonet, leaving his lung agasp –
those minutes watching him sink down slowly into his own blood.
That crib-joint killing in San Francisco:
the black man kneeling, head arced back,
neck wounds bubbling like those
fountains in that Garden of Allah
they show in the magazines.

And then that other time. In France.

The things he'd seen. The things he'd done.

★

Walking faster, nearly dancing now
through the battlefield: with a clip of money
and a book of matches he was looking for fun
or looking for trouble, gasoline
and a body double, a decent drink and a girl maybe,
just looking to get lost –
like how that Chinese place,
The Pacific Shell, on Main and 1st, had lost
the neon for its 'S' and now was a gateway to his world –
and next door to it a bar lousy enough for him,
and he watched
as the cops went in, pulled out a drunk,
smacked him around, and only then, when the heat took off,
only then could he cross the street, push open the door
on the mess he needed.
Blacks, whites, hopped-up Mexicans shouting
to each other over the music:

'Para todo mal, mezcal! Para todo bien, también!'
He got himself some shots and it was all
smeared grins, spilled drinks and sliding eyes
then sudden stand-offs:
'Wise guy, huh? Got something to say 'bout it? Huh?'
Card-sharks and streetwalkers, men out
running drugs and cutting corners,
packing a good piece – blued steel with a walnut stock –
soda-jerks with blades,
kids carrying can-openers – all they could find –
you can't see it but you know it's there.
There's a guy stretched out, in his own puddle,
two others wrestling by the pool table, so drunk they barely move.

His church. His sacraments of whiskey, cigarettes.

A guy loomed up at him, face seamed like a baseball:
'Say, don' I know you?'
'I don't think so.'
'You wanna make somethin' of it?'
'Again – I don't think so.'
'I don' wanna fight you.'
'You're right. You *really* don't want to fight me.'
Scarface flickered then, and blinked:
pushed off from the bar, shouldered his way
muttering through the ruck.

By the pinball machine, down the side of a door,
he saw a pile of emptied billfolds and pocketbooks:
business cards, old railroad tickets, photographs.

And he noticed a girl, over by the jukebox, dancing
on her hindlegs, tipping her toes like a cat
at the end of a rope.

Behind the counter
there was something under a beer crate, turning it
in hard, heavy circles, moving it slowly across the floor.

★

He saw the North Nova's corpse with emptied pockets,
a rifled wallet and a scatter of photographs.

★

He wanted delirium and he wanted it now,
taking a standing drink in any bar he could,
moving through downtown, block by block, through new
blares of neon, streetlights, headlamps,
store-window displays, all
blurred in long exposure: the lights leaving
wavering tracers of red, green,
white gold – like Jackson Pollock
those light trails,
through streams of people, swaying retinal flares.

Main Street, was he on Main?
Every street a one-way street, every alley blind.
This was Werdin Place now, was it? Back of Dreamland,
the Burbank Theater. Too dark to see. Just sit and get a smoke.
Rain had set a gleam into the cobbled stone

that lifted with the ragged light coming in from 5th,
or whatever street it was down there.
The dark compressed, impacted: it had a texture,
granular and grave. It tasted of clinker.
The shadow building hung above him
oblique and sharp as a guillotine blade.
A white splinter cut the alleyway in two: two walls of black
closing on a split world.
Occasionally, a swing of light
arced open

          (a piece of blackness
          goes spinning through)

                         and then closed.
There was something rooting in the bins at the dead-end;
it paused; started again. It came
scampering past, then stopped: light
held in the eyes, green-gold.
He stretched his hand to make it stay
but it never does. The coyote.

                    ★

Downtown was quiet and damp from the fog,
the five-globe streetlights
clicking off as it came to dawn.
He toiled up 4th to Clay past rows of palm trees,
their clumped dead leaves hanging underneath the green
like gray goiters.

In his room, he worked out where he's been
from the match-books in his pocket,

the drinks by the gap in his dollars,
the hole in his life by his eyes in the broken mirror.

★

It rained most days until March: acrid rain
siling down through the smog
that sat there in the low Los Angeles basin like a milky swab.
People went to work in the rain, came home in it:
the bowed heads, shuffling gait of the drones in *Metropolis*.

The raindrops arrowing down and the sidewalk's million mouths
opening and closing for them;
the men's hats and shoulders darkening,
the women's fur coats sleeked like otter pelts.

He went out with Sherwood and Rennert
in their gray Studebaker, with the windshield streaming
and the tail-lights up ahead,
red and guttering, that hypnotic tick of the wipers
swiping *thock, thock, thock*.
Following the trails of the dead,
taking shots of them, telling their stories.
Looking at their corpses, tagged and cold on the pull-out tray:
bloodknots in the hair, still, and a blue
under those eyes that were never quite closed.
Cotton plugging the mouth, nostrils;
the wounds dry, and heavily sewn.
Or that time, in Mercury Court,
down between the Athletic Club and the Warner Theater,
the rain still going – *thock, thock, thock* –

when the cops pointed them on, up the stairs
to the cordoned, unlocked room
and there was this guy sitting against the wall,
like he'd dozed off,
wearing dark-red bib-and-brace dungarees,
an old cigar in his mouth.
They got closer, and saw he was actually naked,
that the thing in his mouth was his cock.

★

Mackintosh took up a Sten gun, shouting, spraying it like a hose at the Germans.
He ran out of ammo, turned back toward us, then we saw how his chest just spat –
then petalled open – and with a great convulsion he flopped down dead.

★

First dry weekend and he's walking, south along the river
– which finally has some water in it now –
trying to avoid those streets dead-ended by the freeways
where the cars slide slowly, nose to tail,
hour after hour, like a production line.
He wanted to see the ocean again, but it was all just concrete:
highways, surface streets, slums, then a toytown called Lakewood,
rows and rows of new identical homes, white homes, then
suddenly, rising up, a mile away,
what looked like a hill covered in trees but couldn't be.
It was oil-wells, lining up on Signal Hill, and more
out east to Huntingdon Beach, and west to Wilmington:
geometric forests right down to the sea –
derricks, pumpjacks, power plants,
mostly tapped-out wells, rusted in the salt air,

160

but hundreds of the jacks still moving, like shore-birds feeding,
dipping their heads to the sand.

★

Back on the Hill, he went to Dr Green's
to get something for his sleeping,
his house and surgery up along Grand by the Frontenac Hotel
a kind of second home for these toothless pensioners
sitting stiffly in his waiting-room, hats on their knees,
chewing on their empty mouths.
They look up at each new patient joining the circle,
half-raising a loose hand in greeting, nodding hello.
He watched each of them, slow and careful, most having
made an effort – brushed their hair, then their shoulders,
checked in the mirror – others long stopped:
rheumy-eyed and shaky; greasy neckbands and stained ties,
cuffs frayed, fingernails broken and black.
If they talked it was about the heat, or their ailments:
bad backs, feet, their joints, cold sores, constipation, teeth –
all waiting to be called by Mrs Green
and shown through the doctor's sliding door.

He got his prescription filled by young Mr Mellon,
bought a paper from Red, standing as usual in his place in the shade,
and saw a woman he recognized, reaching out
with a tremor in her hand
to touch the 'L' of the Lucky Strike sign, for luck.
He went up to the benches to sit in the sun, high over the city.
The news was all about McCarthy, still.
Back in March he'd watched Ed Murrow, taking him down,

right there on television in the Amigos bar,
and then the hearings started
and the army counsel, Joseph Welch, was lifting his sad eyes
to the junior senator of Wisconsin, and repeating,
slow and firm: 'Have you no sense of decency, sir?
At long last, have you left no sense of decency?'

He'd forgotten about the old man, curved as a coathanger,
who walks here every day and only ever sees the sidewalk.
He's hooked as an *r*, a fishing barb,
gnarled and bent
like the thorn on the cliffs of Broad Cove;
each hawthorn tree's baroque twisting
with all the winds' histories worked into it.

The sun hammering back
off the sides of the Alta Vista, and the benches all emptied now,
and no one even out driving, way down there
underneath on 3rd Street,
and the dogs had disappeared: hidden in crawl-spaces, tongues
thick, breathing fast and heavy.
A smell of cheese and brine from the delicatessen,
milk going off in the grocery cans, the metal
too hot to touch, warping, buckling in the heat
so the lids sprung off with a *prang*. The city
trembling below like a gasoline spill.

★

Skid Row was bigger than ever now. The drunks in the park,
curled fetal on benches, or lying out on the dead grass,
almost invisible there

like driftwood on a beach.
Hundreds on the streets out east of Main.
Some jacked on heroin, some plain crazy, most just blown
on Thunderbird, Lágrima de Cristo, Old Monterey.
Flies browsed the broken flesh, sweet smells
hatching from their rags as they turned over, shouting out
at some crime remembered then forgotten,
tongues black from the Gallo wine.

No sign of Velma here, or Billy. But who could tell,
under the coarsened hair, the grime,
they all looked like soldiers painted-up for war.
As someone wrote somewhere: *same faces, different names.*

★

Out with Sherwood and Rennert,
just after Labor Day, over by Union Station,
driving round the gasworks on Ducommun and Center.
Good place for slacking off; good place for trouble.
A few years back, they'd found a circle of girls,
tripped out, cross-legged, naked,
carefully passing around
– instead of a reefer or a pipe – a gray coonhound pup
and its rough tongue, parched and slabbering.
One night, there was a Buick sitting there, under the gas-holders.
Two Indians it looked like, with a shape tied up in the back
and moving; what it was, he couldn't see.

This afternoon there was a film-shoot going –
all the regular stuff, generators, cables, lights on tripods,

camera tracks, grip stands, hangers, wardrobe rails –
and there was Cornel Wilde having a smoke,
talking to this short guy, so they all strolled over, friendly like,
to say hello. Rennert wanted to talk about *Leave Her to Heaven*
and Gene Tierney, so he did,
and the actor was smiling and nodding,
so Walker turned to the other guy,
who said: 'Hi, I'm Joe.'
'Are you in the picture?' Walker said.
'Nah,' he smiled. 'I'm just making it.'
Then it clicked. He'd seen his face in *Photoplay*.
This was the man who shot *Deadly Is the Female* –
Gun Crazy, as it came to be.
This was Joseph H. Lewis.
'How did you shoot that sequence, eh?' he was asking, suddenly,
'Y'know, from the back of that getaway car?'
'Well, son, I'll tell you –
if you tell me a decent bar on Main Street
near the Banner Theater. We're there tonight.'
'Easy. The King Eddy's on the very same block, east on 5th.'

★

It was around seven when he made it over there.
A few older guys at the tables, chewing the fat; some couples.
Nice and quiet.
Till he saw that familiar beanpole at the counter's end,
head down: mantling round a glass and brandy bottle.
The jittering knee. That hank of hair. Pike.
He'd never seen him in here. Didn't even know he drank.

Settling over in a corner at the other end, he waited for Joe
and didn't notice him come in, sports shirt and sailing cap,
even smaller than he remembered. Big grin on his face:
'So howya doing? Walker, right? Get you a drink?'
'Let me, *please*. What'll you have?'
'Just a milk, thanks. Heart attack a few years back.
You believe that? *At forty-six!* Gotta take it easy.'

He had all these questions for Walker: where he was from,
how did he get here, what was he doing.
He was a regular guy. On the level.
'So, you were going to tell me about that getaway scene . . .'
'Okay, yeah. Yeah. Okay: picture this.
You see Peggy Cummins driving toward the bank,
John Dall, shotgun, talking her through it, but behind *them*
five guys, including me, in back of this opened-up Cadillac –
two on top, button microphones under the sunshades,
the cameraman right behind the actors
on a jockey's saddle on a greased plank
– like dolly shots, y'know? –
near three-and-a-half minutes straight through with no cuts,
no re-dubs and *all* ad-libbing.
Jiminy . . . That was *fun*.'
'And the actors?'
'Well, both great, but Peggy Cummins was in charge. Laurie Starr.
She was the soldier Bart never was.
Always ready to kill. Happy to, really.'
Over Joe's shoulder, there was Pike at the bar, eating a sandwich
like he had something against it:
pulling back his head, then lunging in again.
Joe turned to look.

'Say, that kid at the counter,' he laughed, shaking his head:
'Reminds me of a young John Dall!'
'Forget about him,' he threw back his whiskey quickly,
'What about the movie you're shooting here?'
'Well, it's all in the studio really. Chaplin's old set-up
on La Brea and Sunset. Before HUAC drove him out.
We wrapped on the location work today.
Just finished a street scene outside a burlesque. Looking real good.
But we're lucky. You heard of John Alton?'
'Yeah, he's the best: *T-Men, Raw Deal, He Walked by Night*.'
'He's our DP. Got great eyes. *Great* eyes. He can see in the dark
and he's not afraid of it. He's our Caravaggio, y'know?
Wanted to work with him all my life.
This'll be some movie. Hope you like it.
Anyway, pal: glad to meet you. I gotta go. Gotta go.'

Joe walked around Pike at the bar, who
looked up and said something – one word, his name
it sounded like: introducing himself, as always –
before turning back to his drink.
Joe slowed slightly, and stiffened, then
pushed through the swing-door.
Walker knew the word now: it was 'Kike'.

★

A year since he'd seen him, Billy was just sitting there, staring.

One side of him, dirty blond hair down his back, a man shouting:
'. . . I don't even know where the fuck you came from you fuck
you fucking tripped me up you fucker you motherfucker you

what the fuck you doing with that you fucker don't you fuck
don't shoot me don't fucking shoot me fucker don't shoot . . .'

On the other, a black guy with cataracts,
the lenses of his eyes
clouded and blue like distant planets.
In one hand, a photograph, creased,
worn soft and thin as a dollar bill.

A woman, with eight bags of tin cans and the stench of decay.
Her feet wrapped in gunny sacks and a stain
coming through the thick woolen stockings.
Her fingernails were yellow, and scooped liked teaspoons.
'Praise the Lord,' she called out, over and over, 'Praise the Lord.'

And there was a line of kids in their twenties, slow-eyed,
passing the jug of Thunderbird. Back from Seoul with a medal,
a duffle bag and a thirst: a need to get wiped out, to get totaled.
Some had crutches, missing arms or legs; all of them
looking out, like they could see something, straight ahead.

'Howya been, junior?' he said, and started coughing.
He looked ten years older, dragging a little: slow on his feet.
'Yeah, okay, but you're not so good.'
'Reckon I got that valley fever. It's the time of year.
Santa Ana coming in and it all goes to shit.
Get a coffee? Can't do nothin' for them boys right now.'
Walker saw their lips and tongues were already black,
one was asleep, or passed out.

'The old-timers are checking out fast. Now it's soldiers again.
On T-bird.' He took a sip of the terrible coffee.

'But the real thing's the mental jobs, the fruitcakes, y'know.
I can't help those guys. It makes me edgy being around them.
It's driving *me* crazy!' and he laughed, briefly.
'They shouldn't be on the streets, eh.'
'The hell with it,' his smile disappeared,
'*Nobody* should be on the streets.'

He said things weren't so good with the Panama Hotel,
that there wasn't enough room for him and his books,
that he didn't really know what he was going to do.
'But I'll be fine. I'm just a little bushed right now.
And this damn weather gets the whole town jittery.
But how about you, Mr News-hawk?
Still at the paper? Still writing about us?'
'Yeah, still there. I'm doing social issues, the Red Scare,
film reviews now and again, but mostly just city work.'
'You ready to talk to me yet? Y'know, about what happened?'
'Maybe another time, Billy. You're tired, pal;
you look out on your feet.'

★

He heard from a neighbor there was some action outside,
a movie being made around back of the apartments.
He found a crew on Clay Street,
at the foot of the utility steps that run
right behind the Sunshine and the Hillcrest, on up to Olive:
light rigs and mikes and a good-looking actor
sitting in a Corvette, and back of the camera
that big guy with glasses, and the quiet European
with the light meter, from that filming he'd seen

168

at the Nugent deli and the Bradbury Building – three,
three-and-a-half years ago, before he went north.

He'd caught that picture, and it was really good,
the 'M' on the shoulder like the 'M' on the forehead;
and he'd see this new one, no doubt, sometime.
Was he ahead of the rest, or behind? He couldn't tell.

★

Another Christmas on his own.
He found Gitana's number, but it just kept ringing.
The dead rose still has thorns.

He started slow, at the Montana, under the New Grand Hotel.
Got a buzz on with some old guys, then took off downtown.
The Jalisco, with the juicers and barflies,
opposite the cathedral, the Service Club and the Rescue Mission,
then the Indian bars farther down Main – El Progreso,
the Columbine, the Ritz – got a burger at Scott and Freeland
then on to the Torch, double shots half a dollar.
Just to be with other people.

It's 1, 1.30, and he was near the Barclay
when he heard what he thought was some
couple making out – the regular
slap of flesh on flesh and the guttural
huh! uurrh – huh! uurrh – huh! uurrh . . .
The sound of ceilidh night back home.
But then there was sobbing;
he turned round and went down the alley.

This guy, on his knees: rummaging in a bag
it looked like. Then he saw
that his hands were red; and that,
under him, was curled the body of a man.

And now he was on Harlem Place, in back of the burlesques
and the Hotel Rosslyn,
and the next thing he knows it's the girl with the red flower clip:
'Hello, sweetheart. You look lonesome.
You lonesome, soldier?
How's about it? You want a good time tonight?'
'Yes,' he heard himself say.
When they got to the room at the top of the stair
he was hard as coal:
couldn't say a word, just
put a penny in her slot and watched her dance.

★

Through the window, the moon hangs, snagged in the trees;
dogs are browsing through cartons and chicken-bones.
In the corner of the room
the mice on the sticky-trap struggle and die.
Rows of empty bottles. Dead soldiers.
A wife, a home, some kids; none of that possible now.
He took another Seconal, tried to tune the radio
to a station he knew, a language he understood.
From inside the celluloid lampshade, the spider
in his lift-cage rises and falls, rises and falls.
He climbed back into the pill, and sank.

★

The blue buildings step out from the gray, the cool night slipped from
their shoulders like a bathrobe.

December, 54

★

There was a lunch on the Hill that weekend –
'*For those of you alone at Christmas*', the sign said –
in the Bethel Gospel Mission at the foot of Cinnabar Street,
where people went to sing for salvation.
He wasn't going to, but he found himself there anyway.
It was filling up, and there were people there he knew to look at:
one of the barmen at the Montana, a woman from Budget Basket,
Mr Yee the laundryman, a bunch of the old folk
he'd seen standing around. He sat down next to Red, the newsman,
introducing himself.
'Yeah, good to meet you, too. Properly.' Red shook out a Camel.
'Smoke?' In a double-move of his thumb he flicked open his lighter,
clicked down on the flint.
His empty left sleeve tucked into the suit pocket.
'Howdya lose it?'
'Eighth Air Force. We'd caught a load of flak bombing Munich
and crash-landed the way back to Suffolk. Third combat flight,
and the last, obviously.' He smiled. 'And you? You in the war?'
So they spoke about that, joined by an old-timer he'd seen around:
'Say, this is Al. He was in the *first* war. He's got some stories.'
Al talked real slow, but was right on the ball:
'I tell you this, okay: I'm from New York,
was a private in the 369th American Infantry,
but I went to battle in a French helmet.
How about that?
A lot of the white boys wouldn't go near us, y'know,

so we were assigned to the French army.
Kept our US uniforms, but the guns and the rest, they was French.
They didn't mind what we looked like, just glad we could fight!'

Three hours later they were still there, talking,
made a plan to meet up over New Year,
being old soldiers on their own, and neighbors.

★

Al didn't drink, and Red not so much.
He could always cut out later, he thought, but it was fine –
and good to talk about things.

'Dr Green says his daughter comes up here sometimes,
tells him he's crazy paying these prices:
double what it costs in the malls at the Crenshaw Center, or whatever.
But none of us has a car, we walk everywhere, and besides –
we like it on the Hill: the company, the chat, wisecracks, y'know?
Anyway, we've worked out how to shop around for the bargains!'
The Italian coffee machine they were there to try
was hawking up another cup.
'Yeah,' said Al, 'It's like a village in the middle of a big city.
But City Hall and the CRA don't want our village here:
say it's a "blighted area full of drugs and crime and poverty".
They ever been downtown and walked Main Street? The Row?'
'It's the hills,' Red looked up. 'They don't like 'em.
Hills are *inconvenient*.'

They changed the subject back to war, which cheered them up.
The stories of near-misses, wild times on furlough,
the places they'd seen, the *things* they'd seen – being so young.

'I was only scared much later,' Walker said,
and the other two were agreeing, loudly, which was good
because he was shocked he'd said it, right out like that.
'I tell you what I miss, even now,' Al was staring at his hands,
'That closeness, that co-operation, y'know?
In it together, looking out for each other –
what did the Frenchies call it? – *camaraderie*.'
'Yeah. Couldn't sleep for years. No guys with guns in the next bed!'

Outside: the sky, sudden with rain,
and it was pelting down.
They slapped each other's backs and shook each other's hands
and ran.

★

*Under a glower of trees, a frost-pocket. Under the jetty, some thin gray ice
flowered open in places by brittle-stars; on the far bank of Lake Ainslie the brief
sun lights the dead weeping willows like snapshots of fireworks. Under them, the
lathes of ice.*

★

He stayed in for New Year's Eve, as usual, because of the noise.
Rolling pieces of wet paper into earplugs, he sat at the window,
nursing a bottle, watching the lights.
Always reminded him of the tracers – red, blue and yellow –
our guys firing back from the boats
at the planes coming over. The explosions.
He couldn't even hear the splash of whiskey in the glass.

★

173

He heard the telltale click under his boot: he'd triggered a Schützenmine, and when
he lifted his foot a canister of ball bearings would fly up three feet in the air and
detonate. You had to drop quick, coorie in under the blast. So he did.

★

He felt like one of the pensioners, down in Grand Central:
moving slow and careful through the elbowing, jostling crowds,
the calls of the vendors over their cod, lamb brains, cheddar, rutabaga,
him standing there in oddly ill-matched clothes, getting in the way.
The impatient clerks move on to faster customers:
wrapping sausage-meat in waxed paper in a split second,
popping open paper bags with a finger-snap,
twirling them closed with a spin of the wrists.
He's comparing prices, buying almost nothing
and asking for that nothing to be weighed again, on different scales.
He counts out his money slowly from a leather purse.
Lays the package gingerly into the bottom of a giant carrier bag.

He gets his hair cut
down the street at one of the barber colleges.
Feels like a day out.
He tries to remember how old he is. Thirty-four.

★

What had been a blaze of neon, streetlights, lit windows, becomes a
smoldering ruin of blue.

The city is constantly changing, blocks being bought and sold,
demolished and rebuilt, so it has no memory: it knows only this time-
-less present.

What had been a starred canopy becomes squared and defined as a
series of cliffs: a city once more, edged by light.

January, 55

★

He met the old lady again, on the landing, with her shoebox.
'Alfredo not well. He *very* sick boy.' This animal was new,
in a different color, and he couldn't tell what kind of creature it was;
there was a tail and a couple of feet, and the rest was covered
by a sheet of lettuce, moving in time
with the rapid, shallow breathing.

★

The Joe Lewis picture was opening, and he was first in the queue.
The Los Angeles Theater, Broadway, between 6th and 7th:
the best foyer in town for the best-named movie – *The Big Combo*.
Not like his last one, but even better. So great to look at,
it was easy to see Alton in it, hard to see Joe –
and harder to see how it got past the Code.
There was downtown – three blocks from where he was sitting now –
the scene he'd talked about, outside the Banner,
and there were the gas-holders.
Richard Conte perfect as Brown, the syndicate boss.
'I live in a maze,' said Jean Wallace,
'A strange, blind and backward maze,
and all the little twisting paths lead back to Mr Brown.'

He saw its hard lines all the way home through the fog:
the raking headlamp opening up a wall, the shadows
tightening in around this spoon of light that's dragged

175

across the metal doors, snapped back to darkness.
The white verticals tilt and fall,
till they're one long spine of light
through these rainy streets: a needle.

It stayed with him all week, and he went back twice.

★

A month later, the news that Charlie Parker's died. At thirty-four.

★

All the land's been cleared above the Hill Street Tunnel
so it's not even a tunnel, just the double-bore arches:
an empty doorway.

★

The spring trees, somehow, come to bud:
the magnolia, the yellow acacia,
the flowering fruits, apricot, peach and plum.

The children play in the sun on the slopes of the Hill
and the old folk go to the porch,
take their first hesitant steps into the warmth of the day.

★

A raven's thick call; the deer emerging carefully to forage in the first green; the flag iris and fern, the horse chestnut flowering into white candles, the wild lupins and blueberries; some heavy bird uncrumpling from the trees.

★

176

The office at the *Press* is hard to bear.
It's all Pike: Pike who can't stop talking, clicking, talking loudly,
so people think he's alert, hungry, ever-curious, endlessly
moving so we're always dazzled;
he has to stay moving all the time, like a shark has to
keep on swimming or it dies.
Overholt smiles benignly, remembering himself thirty years ago,
not seeing what the others see.
May Wood is blunt about it:
'I hope that kiss-ass chokes on his feed.'

Sherwood and Rennert are reliable company,
Rennert with his stories:
'So there I was in Cole's, with the crowd.
I was asking, and they're giving me quotes – $15 for a broken jaw;
$30 for an arm, a hundred for the whole job – just to see, y'know,
and I'm getting the fish-eye from the guy in the corner, the boss,
and his boy gets a call-down, and he stops,
pats my cheek and says he was only joking, goes back to his seat.
Close shave, I thought.
Then who walks in but Janie from Salaries, y'know? –
tight sweaters and big maracas – and I goes:
"Hey, baby, you look *fine* . . ."
And she's just there, hands on hips, staring daggers.
"C'mon, doll, what say you an' me blow? Know what I mean?"
She's getting in a wax now, starts mouthing off.
I make to leave and she really flips, tearing into me:
"You got some nerve: standing me up last time,
turning up sauced the week before that. My birthday too.
And now I hear you were seen out in O'Riley's on Main
with that floozy from Sales – *Irene Kirchner*, for Pete's sake.

That's it. You and me are all washed up, see? Kaput."
I get myself slapped an' everything. Twice.
The gangsters in the corner, they're cracking up at this,
just pissing their pants and calling out stuff.
But I've just seen a black-and-white pull up outside, you know,
so I go over and I'm calling them chuckleheads, morons, dumbfucks,
then make a break for it – these things, it's *all* in the timing
cause they're scrambling over themselves and piling after me,
this gorilla with a blackjack, couple of bozos slipping on the knucks –
and I open the door onto 6th and say, sweet as you like:
"Evening, officers."
And they look at me, then look at the goon squad,
and they're pushing past,
pulling out their shills and laying into them.'
Rennert closed his eyes and smiled. 'That was a riot, I tell you.
One for the book.'

★

Kiss Me Deadly was what it was called, the one being shot that time
round back of the Sunshine, and the director –
the fat guy with glasses – was Aldrich, Robert Aldrich.
It wasn't just the locations he recognized, this was a movie
about now – that lethal combination of curiosity and greed.
'First you find a little thread,' the girl says.
'The little thread leads you to a string.
And the string leads you to a rope.
And from the rope you hang by the neck.'
The reviews said the lead-lined 'whatsit' they were all chasing
was the Bomb, but he thought it was all about desire:
those desires that will kill or cure us; insatiable, jealous children

178

fighting over Pandora's jack-in-the-box.
When we want everything and give back nothing
the otherworld will be unlocked, and our whole world taken away.

★

He hadn't seen Billy in months, so he went down the East Side;
found him on 5th and Pedro.
He was standing with the one they called Glassface:
half his head disfigured
with a tight, marbled burn,
like his face had melted
all down one side, then frozen.
He'd seen it happen in France, tank guys on fire,
but this was how it looked if you lived.
'Name's Frank,' he said, in a whispery voice,
eyes slightly jumpy.
'Walker. You in the war, right?'
'3rd Armored. The Falaise Pocket.'
'You got caught in a tank, eh?'
'I got caught by the 12th SS, *Hitlerjugend*.
They did this with a trench lighter, trying to get me to talk.'

Billy was standing over him with a cup of water.
'You okay? It was like you passed out . . .'
'Yeah. Yeah, sorry.' He looked around, but Frank had gone.
'Rough story, that – I don't blame you.'
'No. That's not it,' he was up on one elbow,
'They were the ones, Billy, the ones that killed my friends,
other North Novas, boys from C Company,
prisoners they just shot in the head,
or bayoneted, or dragged into the street to be run over by tanks.

I saw some of it, managed to get away, heard the rest after.
I got one of them.' He stood up, brushed himself down.
'Gotta go. I'm sorry, Billy. Now you know.'

★

The Fourth of July. Gun salutes, fireworks. Red, white and blue.

★

Everything in the world opened up behind us. Ships firing a hundred-odd rockets at a time. Woosh! Woosh! Woosh! Woosh! streaming toward the shore, which was on fire. Each flight of rockets sounding like a great sheet being torn apart. Cruisers firing over the destroyers, battleships firing over the cruisers and destroyers and the rocket-ships − all the noise in the world.

I remember looking around thinking: thinking about that hole in the water that's waiting for me.

Checked my rifle again; felt for my watch, compass, grenade, all waterproofed tight in knotted rubbers. We knew the 8th Brigade would already be there on the beach, and we were the next wave behind them following through. The German planes came over and the bullets were raking the hull like hail on a tin roof and we took a hit and the boxes in back of the LST broke open, and out came a spill of white wooden crosses. Grim laughs about that from the boys: how the top brass planned for everything.

I'd always wanted to see France, but not like this. Not this way.

And then, through the smoke, the beach ahead like a sudden city.

★

180

In the midday heat, City Hall looked like itself
reflected in water, glimmering a little
in the waves rising off the asphalt.
A block ahead, the road's flame wobbled into a man, walking,
feet sinking into the black, wading through a puddle of sunlight.

Ninety degrees.

The arches of the Hill Street Tunnel have gone,
along with the hill where he saw *Criss Cross* doubling
and shimmering onto film. Through the emptiness,
the shapes of men waver in the heat, trembling flames that slide,
slow and quivering, long into their own dark pools.

A hundred degrees.

★

*An LBV, and the sea around it, ablaze with a fuel fire. The sunk turrets of
swimming tanks – the DD Shermans – like battle-green islands. On either side,
wrecked boats of the 8th, capsized, blown open; bodies floating face-down in the
sea, nudging each other, their hair moving in the water. Men halfway up the beach
in peculiar, broken-doll positions. The tide coming in on a soldier impaled on a
German tripod, his guts stringing out around him like a kilt. Others hung on the
wire where the weight of their waterlogged packs had dragged and held them close
down into the sand. All these men: waiting so long, to die so fast.*

★

The news on the wire, from Mississippi:
a boy kidnapped from his uncle's house,
beaten and tortured and shot in the head, then

dropped from a bridge, with a seventy-pound piece of metal
tied to his neck with a barbed-wire collar,
into the Tallahatchie River.
Emmett Till, fourteen years old, black.

★

Coming ashore and soldiers in front of me were just slumping down like they
needed a rest. Abrupt trees of smoke and fire. Wounds in the marram, wounds in
the sand. The corporal at my shoulder ran forward, fell, got up, ran forward and
dropped dead – just like a rabbit. We tried to keep moving, tried not to look at the
kids strung up on the lines.

★

Sherwood had picked up something on the LAPD channel,
so he swung the Studebaker across town onto South Central,
way down to 17th, right under the Santa Monica Freeway, the 10,
just empty lots and nothing.
Nothing but a traffic cop pulled in and looking ashen.
They went past him,
under the drumming roar of the freeway and saw it, as if they'd
turned a corner and found a whipping-post, still wet.
The head looked strange – with a flap gaping in the side
like pants with the fly open –
and it was way too big for the body, which seemed flattened.
You couldn't even tell what color he was. If it even was a man.
They'd beaten the blood out of him.
Rennert said he looked like a sock.

★

Arrested in Montgomery, Alabama, for refusing to give up
her seat on the bus for a white passenger –
Rosa Parks was the news in December. 'I thought of Emmett Till,'
she said, 'And I just couldn't go back.'

★

*With high tide and the mass of men and equipment, the Nan White beach had shrunk
to twenty-five yards. All I recognized from the aerial photographs was the big half-
timbered Norman house, all shot to hell. Taken by the Queen's Own and the Fort
Garry Horse a few hours before, the beach was a clearing station now for what was
left of them: their wounded on one side, most with that red 'M' on their foreheads,
for morphine. Farther off, under blankets, the dead stretched out in lines.*

★

Every time he went down the East Side there were more:
Ten blocks of makeshift shelters, tarp and plastic sheets hung
over two-by-fours, men lined up beside them, backs to the walls.

★

There was a minute's silence in the *Press*
for the anniversary of Pearl Harbor.
And there was Pike at the water-cooler, looking at his nails;
looking at his watch.

★

He saw a falling star, that night, through the smog.
He dreamt of his mother, picking him up

183

as a baby and carrying him through all the years
to lay him down here in his grave.

★

He met up with Red and Al when he could,
over Christmas. They hated that time, being alone,
so they talked about anything else,
whether Eisenhower was well enough to run again,
what they thought would happen to Bunker Hill,
but mostly they talked about war.

★

He walked through the city on Christmas Day,
making an inventory of loss: buildings gone,
replaced by parking lots; the buildings scheduled, cordoned off.

★

Building and demolition seem to happen here within the span of a
human life – so citizens can either watch their own mortal decline, or
see themselves outliving their cities.

This is why I miss the island. Nature. We love nature because it dies, and
then comes back to life. A resurrection we can believe in.

December, 55

★

Once Hill Street's hill was re-graded to nothing,
north of 1ˢᵗ Street started falling fast.

They were levelling two blocks between Hill and Grand
for a courthouse;
he could hear the demolition sometimes, inside his room,
taste the dust.
The heating pipes began knocking; leaves
flitted along the floor, but it was January
so they couldn't be leaves,
and were big enough to be rats, but his eyes were wrong:
so ruined now
he would see things, all the time.
The palms outside were black or yellow; nothing's green.
The arms of the geranium, pale, almost transparent,
stretching out to the light.

But there's a bird on a branch, and it's calling.
A bleb in the window-glass
jumps the image
and he sees Annie walking up the 3ʳᵈ Street steps,
but it's just some other woman.

The bird has gone from the branch
but he reconstructs it from its after-image,
what he remembers of its song.

★

*Naked soldiers dead on the beach, clothes blown off by an anti-tank mine. I was
staring at their crew-cuts washed flat by each wave, then the hairs springing back
up. As if they were still alive.*

★

There was one other person in the laundromat that evening
and this man was just gazing, straight ahead
at the wall of machines.
Then he leant forward,
and pointed at the turning clothes, then sniggered to himself
and sat back.
A few minutes later he pulled his chair over, his hands out,
touching the glass of the hot porthole in avid wonder,
watching the moving colors like it's the first television,
breathing, 'Look! Look!'

★

One of the tanks off east to Red beach was in flames, then exploded, and a blown-off hatch-door was suddenly bowling along the sand toward us like a hoop.

★

He was getting his paper from Red when he saw her,
looking twenty years older,
holding on to the Lucky Strike sign like the rail of a roller-coaster.
They helped her to a seat inside the drugstore,
and Mr Mellon gave her a pill with some water.
'She's not sick,' he said later, 'She's homeless.
The CRA just cordoned her street.'

Somebody was ranting on the corner by the Lovejoy:
'Set the trumpet to thy mouth. He shall come as an eagle
against the house of the Lord.' He paused to mop his face,
eyes fixed: 'Set the trumpet to thy mouth!
Pour out your wrath upon them like water.'

★

'Get off the beach!' the Beach Master kept shouting through his loudhailer: 'Keep between the white tapes! Get off my fucking beach!'

On the narrow streets of Bernières, above the landings, there was a crush of tanks, vehicles, bicycles, lines of impatient men, usually stuck behind something broken-down. The weird half-tanks: the Priests, the Crabs and Crocodiles. The locals coming out to greet us with flowers, kisses, calvados. The Glengarries and the Highland Light alongside us, all of us keeping it tight in our squads and platoons. I'd never been with so many people shuffling forward. Bedlam. I hadn't seen the New York subway at rush-hour then, but it was the same.

We got free of it and started moving south to the assembly point at Bény-sur-Mer, clearing as we went. A Fort Garry Sherman took out a pillbox with a shell going straight through the slit. We all cheered. When we got there, there was nothing left but blood and mince. The solid shot had just ricocheted inside, round and round.

★

On 4th and Spring, he saw what remained of the Hotel Angelus
and the Bank of Italy next door. The hotel's whole front side
had come away, so it was like looking into a doll's house,
seven stories high. The wrecking ball was sinking into the brick
and opening up a room at a time, their intimacies exposed.
He could see an ornate roll-top bath, held – rocking
on an edge by its pipework,
a flight of stairs going nowhere, a door
swinging over a sheer drop.
They had hoses playing on the wreckage to keep down the dust
but the air was thick with it,
from the hidden spaces behind walls and ceilings.

He could see part of the basement
under the shattered floor of the great reception hall,
as if a secret panel had been slid aside, revealing
the long white maple lanes of a bowling alley.

★

The sights we saw: cattle lying dead and bloated in the fields, legs in the air; a Panzer tank, brewed up inside, crew done like a Sunday roast; the white horse that suddenly appeared, bolting along the lane, eyes swiveling in panic.

★

Doors open. Crabapple, ceanothus, flowering apricot on the way
through the streets of the Hill, downtown to sit on benches
around the edge of Pershing Square, admiring the new fountains,
reading, talking, in this huge waiting-room,
moving round its clock-face with the sun.

★

The land is closed: by snow all winter, then by the summer trees. We are hidden from sight all year by white or green. The river – coined with light, intricate with the nymphs of the mayfly – is a bed of coiled silver, springs and movements, an escapement of minnows on the face of the water; the long shadows of trout lying like clock-hands under the stones.

★

Pike's ambition was pulling at him like a spring,
winding him in and – with a click – letting him go.

He was really something: a success, always;
anything less was someone else's fault.
On top of it all, right at the top. The top of his game.

★

I remembered the red knot, on their way north in May, how the whole flock
pivots and banks, a coin in the air, like a crowd of people turning to look up,
brown heads lifting to white.

★

The blade-sign reading MASON – HOME OF MEXICAN FILMS
was being levered off the brick, but this was once
the Mason Opera House, where Isadora Duncan danced
in front of fifteen hundred, according to the old guy watching,
and Sarah Bernhardt played – what? – forty, fifty years ago.
As the sign came free of the wall and fell
he turned, and walked away.

★

Aiming for the airport, Carpiquet, we'd cleared Villons, moving south – riding
in carriers behind the Stuart tanks. We captured Buron before noon, then moved
on Authie, half a mile away. Then it all turned. We took casualties under heavy
mortar and machine-gun fire. I was standing in a group of five men and everyone
but me was ripped to shit. Rounds whining off concrete with a puff of dust: bullets
smacked against walls, plugging thickly into the mud; the thump of shells; a run of
slates slithering down; the snicker of rifles.

★

189

The side of a building fell like a tree.
Then the rest of it just collapsed
in on itself, immediately lost
in a dense cloud of brick-dust;
the delay of the noise and shock-waves.
There was an army there, pulling down everything north of 1st.
Behind the wreckers, the power shovels and clamshell-bucket cranes
were lot-grading to street level;
dump-trucks in convoys, shifting all the earth.

★

We sheltered in a half-ruined house for a few hours, to get chow and some shut-eye. Upstairs, we found a perfect closed room of Murano glass, vitrines of painted miniatures, tiny gold icons. Looking out the window to the courtyard below there was a small girl lying in the shape of a star, in the center of a pool of russet.

Then the Germans found our position there in the southwest of the town, and hit us with 88s and mortar fire. The sound of mortars like gravel on a metal slide; a running tear. Right next to me, young Benjamin took some shrapnel in the throat: his windpipe torn open, so he's gargling blood and staring at me, fumbling at his neck like he feels his napkin is slipping.

★

The scrape and whine of metal on stone. The drumfire of falling buildings.

★

Things went wrong quickly. We couldn't seem to get any artillery back-up, and the few Sherbrooke tanks we saw arriving got nailed by 88s. Seemed we'd pushed

190

too deep and got ourselves flanked, so Captain Fraser was told to dig in on high ground in an orchard above Authie. We had three Brownings stripped from Shermans; one remaining tank. We could see the Germans in Franqueville waiting to attack. But they could see us too, or somebody could, and soon enough we had their big guns coming down on our position. We'd dug slit trenches, gun emplacements in under the trees, but there was nowhere to go when the 88s hit: percussive shock-waves like punches, the thunder-shocks under the boots, and we were digging with our helmets, our hands, trying to make holes for our soft, unsafe bodies. The ground up ahead rose heavily, like a wave, and broke on us in dirt and stones.

★

The rubble chutes were constant thunder: from the top stories to the dump trucks, from Hill on up to Grand. Façades of buildings breaking off, snapping like the icing on a cake. The whole thing watched with interest by men looking down from behind the barriers on Bunker Hill Avenue, like it was a newsreel.

★

A soldier walking behind our line, like a sleepwalker, a fence-paling gone right through his chest.

There was a huge hit to the left of my trench; the shock-waves knocked me over on my back and I took all the stones and mud before something the weight of an ammunition pouch landed square on my gut. I couldn't see through the smoke, but when I reached down I found I was holding something warm and familiar: a human hand.

★

Cranes with caterpillar tracks shuddering over the rubble, pulling down the world.

★

You could see the Panzer Mk IVs coming on with their 75mm guns, and these
– we knew – were the SS, the Hitlerjugend. The ping of bullets now, above the
shred and crump of shells. Geysers of earth going up around us – brown, gray,
occasionally a sudden red. The thrown helmets, wet rags of flesh, the sharp stench
of liquid shit you just found with your foot. Next to me, Douglas was shot in
the mouth and went down, Sergeant MacPherson was sitting, waving his hands
frantically, twisting round, looking for help, mad eyes like a mother with a dead
baby; his legs underneath him bent awkwardly, completely still.

Those that could walk were told to withdraw with Lieutenant Veness before the
circle closed. Jimmy Millar stood up to go, then snapped shut like a knife and didn't
move again. We pulled back, leaving Captain Fraser and a handful of men. I felt
something tug at my shoulder, and the wetness.

★

The lake darkens, and the surface breaks once, to the pull and cheep of an otter
reaching shore, and twilight deepens, erasing every tree; then only the birds
remain, the long mournful wail of the loons calling to each other, all through the
blue of the night.

★

Red told him Dr Green had died.
That he'd been the doctor of Bunker Hill for nearly thirty years,
would only take what you could afford;

192

paying it himself if he had to.
'What will Elizabeth do now?' he said. 'What will any of us do?'

The Holy Joe across the street is scratching his head, expressionless,
swinging round and pointing:
'Set the trumpet to thy mouth! The king is cut off.
The king is cut off, as the foam upon the water.'

★

This time Billy wasn't wearing a Santa Claus hat,
but a leather flying helmet and a necklace of dog tags.
He looked done in.
He raised a hand in what seemed like a greeting
but it was to touch his face lightly,
and he saw then that the hand held something, a tiny penknife,
that he'd drawn it
slight above an eyebrow
making a line of small red beads.
'Keeps me awake,' he said.
This close, he could see now
his face was cross-hatched like a wood-engraving.
Billy reached out
and he felt a brush on his cheek
then the smart.

★

*My shoulder wasn't too bad once I patched it up, but I'd got separated from
the rest. Thought I'd try to make it back to the house in town with the glass and
the icons, the girl in the pool of blood. The streets were full of the dead, and sounds*

of men running, so I pushed through the first ruined door I found, and climbed what remained of the stairs to the top. Half the roof had gone, but I could see out from three sides, including what looked like the main square, out front — almost empty, with just a handful of civilians getting field-dressed by a medic.

★

Spooked by seeing Billy like that, with all those fucking tags,
he took the Red Car to Venice, to the city's rim,
the city dying all the way to the sea.
He walked through Windward Avenue, deserted in January
except for rough sleepers and junkies,
through the oil derricks and pumpjacks
and along the canals with their shopping carts, gondolas and trash.
And on, through a thin rain, down to the beach, looking south
to the treatment plants at Marina del Rey:
black cylindrical tanks and sewer-pipes,
working overtime to fill the sea with Kotex,
straggling there like jellyfish,
or glazing the beaches with condoms: all
perished now to circles, frail as honesty.

Nothing on the sand but the sweat of death.
What's left of a humpback, forty-foot long,
one pectoral fin stretched up like a sail, its grooved runners
a grounded boat, tipped over.

★

Original cities were contained, concentrated social collectives. But Los Angeles is the opposite. Immune to everything but the limits of its host,

the city expands at pace – to the edges of its territory: the mountains, its
neighbors, the ocean's verge – an infestation, a carcinoma.

January, 57

★

In the papers next morning: Bogart is dead.

★

Everything on 1st and Olive is emptied,
taped off, ready to be demolished.
Now they're working south where the ground starts rising there,
busy on the roof of the Union League Building, 2nd & Hill,
across from Hotel Astor.
A pincer movement.

★

*I must have slept, because I came to with a jump. A lot of shouting below at the
back and there's one of our boys with his hands up. Then the sound of two shots,
and he's down. There was a firefight out front, on the square, with the Germans
blazing away at a church. I could see a Canadian stretched out, bleeding from a leg
wound, his rifle ten feet away. It looked like Bill Nichol, of all people, and I was
pleased to see him moving, trying to get up. I watched as an SS officer went over,
picked up Bill's rifle and stoved in his head with the butt – three, four times – then
finished him off with a single round.*

★

The whole block on 1st Street, west of Olive, has gone,
and they're working the other side of the street,
east toward Olive Court and the Gladden.

★

They had numbers on the square now and there were prisoners coming in from all sides, under escort; armored cars, troop carriers, motorbikes with side-cars, and swastika flags going up on what was left of the buildings. I had my Lee–Enfield, with three magazines, a Fairbairn–Sykes fighting knife and, somewhere, a bayonet.

I tried to make out the regiments of the prisoners, and could see some Cameron Highlanders, Sherbrookes, a few Queen's Own and Winnipeg Rifles, then a row of North Novas, it looked like. Then I spotted Tommy Davidson and John Murray and maybe six others from C Company, in bad shape but alive, sitting under guard. Some SS men went over, real hitchy, wired-up and shouting something at the men. I saw the prisoners look at each other, slowly taking off their helmets, and then they were all jerking and slumping to the rattle of the submachine guns.

★

The four-ton wrecking ball had opened up one whole flank of the El Moro Hotel, and showed the inside walls of twenty rooms, without floors or ceilings now, each with their different wallpapers, brighter where a picture or a cupboard once had been.

★

The Hitlerjugend, laughing, dragged two of the bodies into the middle of the street – hoping for traffic – and I could hear their giggling drowned out by the rumble of tanks. After the Panzers went through, the villagers were allowed to take the bodies for burial: scraping them off the cobblestones with a shovel. Tommy Davidson, who worked on the coal in Stellarton, Nova Scotia.

★

The ball and giant claw were eating their way through the corner of Hill and 1st, and after El Moro there was the Moore Cliff Hotel –

halfway up the hill – clearing the ground of places to live, in exchange
for places to park.
Olive Court had disappeared. The entire 100 block on South Olive
nearly gone now; just the Gladden Apartments, where Chandler once
stayed, still there on the corner, empty.

★

*I saw one of the dead boys, I couldn't tell which; he'd been propped up, an old hat
tilted on his head, and what looked like a cigarette packet stuffed in his mouth.
Everything below his chin, bright red.*

★

The Gladden was pulled down, and that was the whole block gone.
A scoop shovel moved across its remains, scraping it up into trucks.

★

There's a guy at the bar on his own:
Steve, or Sam, he said his name was.
You could tell he was big, even sitting down;
spit of Lawrence Tierney.
Blood through one eye like the twist in a marble.

This old doll at the other end of the counter, the look
of fallen masonry about her: face
a ruin of crumbling plaster, badly painted,
eyebrows halfway up her forehead, her mouth
like it'd been dug out with a knife.

Walker threw back a shot, watching
as the room started filling up.
There was a guy called Stan in the corner
with some mark and a set of cards,
running the old gypsy switch, jazzing the chump.
Some couples were in, and three babes
at the table by the door, all hair and hands, laughter.
Such girls:
you could hardly look at them, they were so bright.

Steve, or Sam, was talking to the bar-keep:
'I'm nobody's friend, the man with no place.'
'Sure, bud. Same again?'
The old dame's just staring at the bottles behind the bar,
the reflection in the mirror, lifting another gin.

The three by the door were getting louder.
One of the girls says to one of the others:
'So he's hitting me up for a loan. *Me*, without a red cent!'
'Didn't he just put a ten-spot down on the Rams to win?'
'Yes!' Her voice was going higher, her head moving up and down.
The third – blonde hair cut like a boy – isn't listening,
she's just turning around, all smiles.

Sam, or Steve, was pulled tight as a rubber band, getting into a beef
with a couple young punks that end of the counter:
too close for his liking.
He's getting sore
but they're too dumb to notice.
They'll learn, next time,
to be cautious of someone with nothing to lose.

He's looking straight ahead, through the bottles and the mirror:
going quiet,
like a pan about to boil.
He stood up from his stool, tossing back his whiskey, winced, and
turning to the first guy
dropped him with one punch;
smacked the other's face onto the bar,
splitting his nose in two,
slung a dollar down and walked out the door.

The only sound was the old girl
fumbling open the clasp of her purse
and throwing up inside.

The blonde's at his shoulder, suddenly,
with her pixie eyes. 'Will you buy me a drink?
I'm Lily. I'm a neighbor. I live at the Hillcrest Hotel.'

★

The open cupola of the Seymour Apartments no longer looks out
over the steel frame of the courthouse.
The new concrete of the courthouse
looms over what was once the Seymour, levelled that afternoon.

★

*The flush of wind on the sea, the slap of rain-squalls over MacDonald's Cove.
All the snapped trees, jackstrawed in a tangle. Then that quick sun after rain,
brighting the gold of the lichen, the new ferns, the water pooling there in the
rocks.*

★

He walks through ruins. Stained glass, turned wood,
exquisite broken tiles. Finds, in the dust, a chest spilling open
its museum of everything that's gone.

★

*That special drawer in the dresser that Mother called the glory-hole: blunt
pencils, tickets, paperclips, perished rubber bands. Milk-teeth, keys, apostle spoons,
instruction manuals. Ribbons, receipts, half a school report card, a birthday-cake
candle. Three playing cards, four empty envelopes, rosary beads, photographs of
strangers. All fallen through the cracks to this limbo of the lost, like all those
mornings believing in the tooth fairy or Santa Claus, the years wasted on hoping,
the years spent spinning gold back into straw.*

★

The Richelieu goes the next afternoon, and then
her beautiful neighbor, the Melrose Hotel.
The wreckers have reached 2nd Street, one block away.

★

*I'd seen enough, decided to get out of there that night, clear the town and push
north-east: try and reach our lines.*

*The SS were in festive mood, singing out on the square that was all lit up by the
flames from the burning church, and the line 'Und morgen die ganze Welt' was
shouted again and again. Slipping out the way I'd come, I was quickly beyond
Authie, through backstreets and into the fields – avoiding the Buron road and
its occasional headlights, and stumbling on through a muddy darkness lit by a
quartered moon. I nearly ran right into a German patrol, so dropped, fast, into*

what felt like a crater. There was that familiar sweet smell and then that deep and dissipating snore that I knew was a death-rattle. Something was moving, across from me in the dark. Under the brief, dead light of a magnesium flare, I saw the bodies lying there: odd parodies of human beings. Four men in khaki; three gone for sure. One fell open with a touch of my boot. I couldn't tell with the fourth one, but I found a morphine syrette and gave him a shot. Threw some sulfa powder into the wounds in his leg. When the light came up I could see he was a North Shore and not going to last. I lit a cigarette for him, watched the smoke stream from a hole in his chest. 'You gotta stay off the Cussy road,' he was gasping, 'I saw them killing prisoners, so don't take any of them. Remember Dieppe.' He coughed a little blood then and, as if embarrassed to be dying, covered his face and went still.

I heard the wheezing of mortars and could gauge the progress by where the smoke cauliflowered up; making out the lines of engagement now, seeing where the road was. The heat from the morning sun had woken the corpses around me, starting their soft gurgling, the occasional slow hiss.

★

Half the Hill was down with valley fever: shortness of breath,
fatigue, headaches, a rash of red bumps on the legs, night sweats.
They say the building dust was full of spores.

Cistus, pink bougainvillea, night-blooming jasmine,
white hibiscus, azaleas, daylilies, red and yellow oleander.
He walked past all the gardens he knew, just to breathe again.

★

Al had borrowed this old beat-up Pontiac for the day,
filled the back seat with bottles of water, a pack of sandwiches,

201

and they made their way up to Sunland
to the foothills of the San Gabriels, then on to the trailhead.
The air was already clearing
as they found the sign for Mount Lukens,
at the start of the Stone Canyon Trail.
It was hot, though, even at nine in the morning,
and the climb was stony and hard, so they found excuses to stop.
'This is nothing like the high ground I'm used to.'
Al knew these mountains, had walked them for years:
'I guess this is pretty different.
We're, what, fifteen hundred miles south?
Mostly chaparral up here in the Gabriels, the whole region,
it's all that survives the heat and the wildfires:
yucca, manzanita, ceanothus, chamise,
deerweed, scrub oak, sagebrush, yerba santa.
The only big trees we'll see are Californian live oaks, Douglas firs.
Now, if you can find any soil in among all those rocks,
feel what it's like.'
He bent and picked up a handful and it was a powder,
dry as crushed leaves.
'That's why these mountains burn. That's the fuse.'

They got to the top of Mount Lukens around noon,
Los Angeles stretched below in its heavy haze.
Al shaded his eyes from the sun:
'You can see why the Indians called this "The Land of Smoke" –
looks like it's *already* on fire.'
Walker had seen things like this before: battlefields, cities destroyed.
There was the glinting twist of the river-bed, City Hall of course,
and then south to the port, and Catalina Island;
he could make out the top of Bunker Hill,

Chavez Ravine maybe, that was all.
Soon it would just be the dead river and City Hall.
'No Indians now, eh,' he muttered, 'Except on Skid Row.'
He was hot from the climb, but felt
he could breathe now, in the free air,
up above it all, and see more clearly: the city
tied up below in its meshwork of highways and roads.

They had lunch in the shade of some boulders.
'You see these mountains around us?
They're sitting on fault lines that've been shifting
and slipping for centuries, grinding them up.
Under this mantle of chaparral and scrub
the rock's already shattered:
it's like gravel in a paper bag.
When the chaparral burns in the fire season
all these mountains will be ready to go.
The debris flow will be unbelievable: like glaciers calving.
If we get a real earthquake, the Big One,
with the Santa Ana fire-winds blowing:
that, my friend, will be it.
The city'll burn, right back down to the sand.'

★

*From the trench I was in, it sounded like the rush and splash of water over rocks,
but it was the crush of flames, raging, snapping at old wood and the grenier was
collapsing with a last parched roar, and the rippling spray of sparks and smoke.
A red river, pouring itself out into a gray hearth.*

★

The winds were in from the north–east, hot and dry;
a yellow cast to the light.
He felt that mood on the street, that tension, the stillness
just before the riot.
His sight was wrong. There was a shiver and slip
out of the corner of his eye. The running dark.

★

You had to look people in the eye during combat, to check they understood an
order; that they were fully engaged, committed to carrying it out.
The same with the men who were dying: the soldier with his jaw blown half-off,
trying to hold it in place.
The men you killed. You had to look them in the eye too: see the life dimming
there as they died.

★

The old lady on the stair where he lived
was standing in her doorway, looking around.
'Alfredo – he gone.'
She showed him the inside of the shoebox:
just a coin of carrot and some scat.
Stared up, imploring: 'Where he go? Where he go?'

★

I got back to our lines, having seen the disintegrating bodies in the ditches, guys hit
by heavy guns, filleted by the shock. And what the SS had done on the road: lines
of men with head-shots.

I was sent east through a wood to link up with some other North Novas. There,
hanging from a tree, was a German: dancing all wrong.

★

The treetops are swaying, but there's no wind.

★

Pike was always in a movie, the cameras always rolling;
he sweeps his hair from his eyes:
long shot, close-up, man of the moment –
roving reporter; editor in waiting.

★

Birds broke from the trees, in every direction.

★

'*Yeah-yeah-yeah,*' was his machine-gun way of saying:
Look, I know all this. I'm a busy man.

★

Outside on the line, a white shirt on a wire hanger begins to dance.

★

Pike carried a pen with him
wherever he went – in his mouth

or behind his nonchalant ear or
clicking at his side as he strolled down the corridor
– just to show he was ready,
always, for important editing.

★

The wind had set a tinkling going through the telephone wires,
but there was no wind.

★

The city is held in balance: always unfinished, always being demolished.
If the construction and destruction ever stopped, the city would fail.

City Hall is a black obelisk in first light, till the sun finds a purchase on
the face of the stone and light peels open one side.

A bedroom door, coming ajar.

The rasp of a dagger being drawn.

November, 57

★

He stayed in for New Year, as always,
watching the fire through a bottle;
walking out, after everything was done.
Wading through shadows, now,
the streets possessed by ghosts.
Cities are a kind of war, he thought:

206

sometimes very far away then, quickly, very close.
The smell of smoke and cordite,
the blackened, empty shells of rockets cooling on the stones,
the trash of a thousand street-parties, the spent bodies. It was like
swimming through canals of broken glass.
A tunnel under a hill: stretching on forever to an unblinking eye,
bright and blind.
Then the shadows tightened and closed to lamp-black
with that whir: the granular
sheathing of a camera's leaf-shutter.
The way the dark
looked like it was being worked at
with multiple blades of light,
carving out pieces of the frame to silhouettes
of scalpel, cleaver, scythe, then
clicked off
and started again
with a splash of white
across the brick of a wall,
a skewer, or thorn through the packed darkness
and it's moving down, sudden, under him
and he can make out the light of a door opening:
a false floor, scaffold hatch, a dead-drop
falling away.

★

Red was there, in his place on the corner
by the drugstore, 3rd and Grand.
'Elizabeth Green just died.
Y'know, Dr Green's widow?

Sweet lady. Very sad. They'll pull down their house, I guess,
now they're both gone.'
'Well, it's what Mayor Poulson talks about, isn't it,
one of those "little illegal hovels" attracting crime and squalor.
And, anyway, we *really* need another parking lot.'
Red took a deep breath, shook his head:
'Three blocks of downtown went last year.
They're not stopping, y'know?
The Hill, between Temple and 2nd; it's all cleared now.'
He looked north.
'I guess we're next.'

★

The scent of wisteria in the air, which he traced
down Bunker Hill Avenue to number 325, the Castle.
Must have been planted when the house was built,
eighty years ago, this beauty: trunk like a tree now,
the whole southern side, cascading violet-blue.

★

Down 3rd to Main: houses boarded up, stores
with their windows soaped over, signs saying **CLOSING OUT SALE**.
Breaks in the street where buildings had been,
being cleared for parking lots.
On the East Side, the beat cops were out, their authority
swinging on their belts in leather holsters,
whirling their night-sticks like propellers, moving in pairs
through the desolation, the shanty town of rags and cardboard,
shaking down dealers, beating the tar out of any trouble.

He saw Glassface on the corner of Boyd and Los Angeles,
rolling a smoke by the shut-down pawnbroker's.

'Hello, Frank. I'm Walker, friend of Billy's.'
Frank studied him for a moment. 'Yes, I remember.' He smiled:
'We got the 12th SS in common, don't we?'
An old woman scuffed past, crusted sores at her mouth,
feet in blue plastic bags.
'How is he?'
'I'll level with you. Billy's been out on the street too long.
He's shot to hell. Got bounced from the Panama with all his books.
That's bad enough, but he owes some people some money
and they're gonna take him for the gold in his teeth.'
'Where is he? Usual place, eh?'
'Nah, the cops ran him in for his own safety.
He's in the tank for a couple nights.
Say, could you use a coffee?'

'The 12th SS killed a whole bunch of prisoners, right? Canadians?'
'180 at least, they think. Hard to tell, y'know.
All straight after the breakout from Juno; three, four days.
All of them prisoners of war.'
'We ran into them straight after that. In Falaise.
Reckon they were popped on bennies, y'know: antsy,
mad eyes; some even frothing at the mouth. They never slept.'
'How *could* they sleep? I saw some of what they did.
Heard the rest years later. They deserve anything they got.'
'I see what they did every day,' Frank closed his eyes,
'Just wish I could get even.'
Walker looked down, as if he'd dropped something:
'I did.'

'Meaning what?'
'I got one of them.'

★

He dreamt he was back in Broad Cove, in the church hall, on ceilidh night – that, one by one, the uniformed men stepped out of the shadows: ten, twenty, a hundred, a thousand; standing there till the dark closed over everything but their held-out hands.

★

'Hello, Lily. Can I get you a drink?'
In daylight she looked like a damaged bird
in her little black-and-white dress;
you could see the hunger-traces, the lines of trouble
fret-marked on each wrist.
You could picture her as a young girl,
cutting out the imperfections on her arms and legs
with a razorblade,
so in this long sunlit Hill Street bar they flashed,
those dull flat scars, like slubs in silk.
'Sure. I'd like a gin sling please. A nice big one.'

He thought he saw Gitana in the crowd, but she'd be in Boardner's
or Scandia or the Formosa by now, collecting celebrities
in her little book: remembering everything, manipulating
everything. Knowing nothing.

Some guy leant over and muttered in his ear:
'Don't tangle with that broad, fella. I'm tellin' ya.

210

She's a hot number, sure, a straight knockout,
but she'll do you like a .30-30.'

'What did he say to you?'
'Ah – don't know. Couldn't hear.'
'He's a sleazebag. A schmo, that guy, I tell you, a *real* schmo.'
'Okay, okay, don't blow a fuse!'
'*Feeblo* . . .'
'Here's your drink, Lily.'
'Thank you.' She gave herself an anxious little hug,
lifted her chin, then looked him in the eye, went back to talking
in that sleepy way he liked.
'I'm sorry. It's my nerves. You're a regular guy; a *helluva* guy,
whatever your name is . . .' She giggled, 'A real dreamboat.'
'Let's drink to that,' he smiled. 'Keeping ourselves afloat.'

★

Under the opened trees, the night's colander of stars, the wave reached deep into
itself – shook with a rattling sound, and withdrew, leaving gifts on the long shore.

★

The hooked nets, the scuffles of desire.
Ridden by lust, and then being rid of it:
the shallow urgency, interminable regret.

★

Strange smooth things beached here: a pelvis of tree-root, panels of wooden fish-
crates from Mallaig, Kirkwall, Bantry Bay, a lead-lined box encased in leather,

211

glass floats in blue and green. They lay, listening there to the night waves, the
slow chafe of the ocean breaking.

★

He thought she was asleep
but she turned over in the bed
and he could hear her voice,
see her eyes, bright:
'Hey . . . hey, I got this . . . you know, I got this ticking noise . . .'
'Yeah, okay.'
'No, really . . .'
'Good night.'
'. . . this *ticking* noise in my head . . .'

★

He woke suddenly and turned around, but the door of the dream had
closed behind him. Scrabbling at the surface he could find no handle, no
handhold, to let him back in to his childhood, to the bar at the end of
the world.

★

No sign of Overholt at the *Press*
so he handed Miss Briggs his last bulletin on the homeless,
then went to the bar on 2nd and Spring
to look for Sherwood and Rennert.
Through the cigarette smoke he could see them,
sitting in their favorite booth, and there was Pike
who'd watched him walk in

and had set it going – what he'd planned as a smile – playing now
round his mouth, like a fly around a wound.
He had his pen in one hand, and was snapping the end of it
in and out, in and out: *click, click, click.*

So he kept on walking,
straight past the booth and out the side door.

★

He went to Cole's, saw a face he knew
through the crowd at the bar.
Black curls and glancing eyes, Gitana, the Mexican,
with her cigarette and glass as always, ready for her close-up,
but jowled, and huge.
A caricature of before, she looked like nothing on earth.
Hank Quinlan in a skirt.
There was no part of her
you could have touched that wasn't fat.
Her forehead perhaps.
He turned on his heel and left.

Two bars without a drink.
He stopped at the first dive where he could hear the bright *tink*
of music, a gulping beat when the door swung open.
He ducked in, under the sign:
the neon sizzling like a nest of crickets.
There was room at the counter, so he pulled up a stool,
called for a rye and looked around.
A lit box sat up on a shelf above the bar
with black fish-shapes stalled there,

drifting, darting sometimes, in its gray,
which he realized, after a while,
was a television ball-game.
Next to it, an advertisement for Lucky Lager:
It's Lucky When You Live in California.
'Same again.'
He was trying to pace himself, but it wasn't working
and he wasn't feeling too lucky.
'Get a load of them two honeys! Some build on that blonde, ay?'
'Yeah, a real dish. The brunette, though! Like my meat *dark* . . .'
They were just two jerks with a load on,
but he couldn't stop himself; he looked over.
Let the first one *see* he was looking.
'What's griping you?' the kid says, with his chin out.
'You're crowding your luck, sonny,'
taking out his Fairbairn–Sykes and laying it gently on one knee.
'If you want to hang on to that little cock of yours
I'd leave now, quietly, out that door.'

A few more whiskeys and he felt his shadow catching up
so he steadied himself to leave; saw an old man
right in front of him doing a strange, stiff shuffle,
shifting his weight from foot to foot,
not knowing where to put his hands, as if he'd discovered
the pockets of his jacket were still sewn up.
Then he sees it's himself, in a mirror.

Outside, the ground slewed under him,
yawing and dropping
like he'd stepped down into a canoe.

There was a blur of neon as he fell,
headlong, into his own shadow,
a shadow the length and breadth of him.

The city was watching. He got up. Walked.
When he stopped, so did the footsteps,
so he couldn't stop: he just had to keep moving.

A few lights still on.
Hall lights shining through the stained-glass windows,
each porch a tiny sunset.

Having finally found a home, a home on the side of a hill
– an acropolis on the brow of the city –
they were pulling it down.

He's like the faded lettering on buildings, old advertisements
for things you can't buy, that aren't made any more:
ghost signs.

★

The coyote was watching.
Tail bushed open – held straight out.
In its eyes, the stolen fire.

★

The house-lights went up, and it was morning.
He needed to find Billy, if they'd let him out of the cooler by now,
so he threw some water on his face and started downtown.

A thick gray smog, the palm trees black
with carbon from the tunnel,
black leaves rotting on the ground: husks scattered
like small boats for the dead.

He had to finish telling Billy what he'd done, back in France.
It was eating him up. Eating him alive.

Hill, Broadway, Spring, Main, the streets almost empty;
4th, 5th, Los Angeles, Wall, the sidewalks lined with men.

★

Was this how it was?
Skid Row, 5th and Pedro,
emerging, riveled and gray,
from his tent of sacks and cardboard,
papery torso like a wasps' nest,
a wizened man with perfect teeth,
who bares them, shadow-boxing with his little fists,
shouting, 'I'm Billy Idaho!
I'm as strong as ever!'

★

Or had he been reading under his streetlamp? Eyes always
darting around, checking the bundled men on either side,
scanning the intersections, watching for strangers,
patrol cars, changes in the light.

★

Or bent over, tending to Velma's impetigo or leg ulcers;
cleaning and drying the wounds of all the broken soldiers.

★

No. It was this: Billy Idaho
in his own shirt of body-lice and scabies,
back to the wall
on his board and blankets,
with his precious books
on the corner of 5th & Pedro,
when they came and set fire to him.
And he just sat there,
in his favorite place on the street,
batting at flames like they're flies.
Ten minutes
and there was nothing left to see of him but his teeth.

'Lanciatore says hello,' one of them had murmured.

They came back to check
and then burned his books,
from which
large flat ashes
were lifting
up into the air.

He stood across the street
where they landed on his skin
like black butterflies.

217

He kept seeing those last moments
in negative, a blaze of black,
the effigy on the bonfire
sagging in the flames.

All the things in that man's head:
the things he knew, what he'd seen in his life.
And that body: what it had gone through all these years;
what his hands had done, had learnt to do.

★

He had no idea where he was. He was just walking.
And so why was Pike there – Pike, of all people –
there on the corner, with that grin, and his Zippo, clicking away?
'Ahhh . . . best smell in the world,' he said, sniffing theatrically.
'Barbecued nigger.'

★

'You have sown the wind . . .
You have transgressed, and trespassed.'
The boy in the blue suit was repeating, soft and low,
'. . . Transgressed and trespassed. An east wind shall come.
The wind of the Lord shall come up from the wilderness.'

★

He remembered her long fingers, cool at his neck.
Her clean, blue eyes.

★

218

Where has kindness gone,
and tenderness
and gentle hands
inside this fire,
among these many blades?

The boredom of childhood, out on the island,
those endless days
when nothing happened.
Now he couldn't keep up – the years
hard-hammering shut behind him.

No one knows where I am, he thought, or what I'm doing.
'And now,' he said out loud to the mirror,
'I can't make myself reappear.'
He tried to slide the loose half back into place
but it broke off in his hand.

He'd drowned his looks.
His mind:
shot to pieces, now, but every single image still there, complete.
If only he could lose them too; if he could drain them out.
If he could only drain his eyes of all they'd seen.

★

There was a juddering, like a freight train coming through,
and the ceiling light started swinging, gently.
His eyes shivered out of focus at the pile of books, toppling.
He looked down at the water in the basin which was moving.
And then it stopped.

Smoke in the air as he walked up 3rd to the Alta Vista,
along to the Dome. He could see fires up north in the mountains:
orange chains in the dark, like the high ground north of Falaise.
His Fairbairn–Sykes resting in its sheath on his belt
as he made his way down.

Through the fog and smoke, the city below like a sudden beach
in flames: flares of neon wavering in the night's heat,
winks of light from the parked cars down on Hill and 3rd.
The rumbling roar behind him sounded like the hill collapsing
but it's the clatter of the Angels Flight reaching dock.

Glassface – Frank – he would get it, he'd understand.
Pushing in and drawing it out, reaching back
to pocket the glimmer.
After all the bullets and shells, there was something so intimate
about stabbing a man.

The ground flinched again, and people staggered slightly, hands out
for balance, looking around for the source.
The blind balloon-seller, outside the Broadway Department Store,
lost his footing and one pink balloon, which drifted away east
through the yellow light down the long channel of 4th Street.

Something was going on, out in that direction, south of City Hall:
sirens, smoke and blowing embers, then flames, jumping
through hot air; ambulances, fire-trucks with ladders.
Above it all, the police helicopter
hanging there like a wasp.

Each temblor set the birds flying in all directions, the people
like civilians under heavy fire, white-eyed, crowding,

moving in fits and starts, staring around them.
He ducked down a service alley, weaving his way
to the East Side, where nobody would care or even notice.

It took an hour to find him, and he looked like he'd been waiting.
He pulled out a pint of rye and Frank had his white port
and they raised their bottles to toast him, their dead friend.
He couldn't look at Frank – who had tears standing in his eyes,
his mouth moving. He just said to him, 'I've come to confess.'

★

'We knew a lot after Caen, moving south to Falaise.
There was an abbey the Germans used as a field HQ,
south-east of Authie. You know Panzer Meyer, right?
Yeah: course you do. Kurt Meyer was in charge:
commander of the 12th SS Panzer Division, *Hitlerjugend*.
That was their name.
They were shooting their prisoners. I saw them doing it.
Turned out they killed twenty Canadians in that place alone.
Twelve were North Novas. I was good friends with six of them:
George McNaughton, Ray Moore, Jimmy Moss,
Hughie MacDonald, Hollis McKeil, sweet Charlie Doucette.
Just lined them up. Back of the heads.'
He took a deep pull on the bottle.
'So we were after revenge – after Meyer most of all –
and we thought we had him in the pocket, the Falaise Pocket, eh,
but he got away. Only did eight years, y'know.
They let the bastard out in '54.
They didn't *all* get away, though. Oh no. I got one. With this.'
He lifted his shirt to show the Fairbairn–Sykes in his belt.

When he started to talk, his voice went flat,
like it wasn't his anymore.

★

He looked up, when he was done, and Frank was staring at him,
shaking his head. 'You see *here*?' he said, turning
to expose the tight gray side of his face, all raised
like a puddle of dirty ice. 'You're no better than them.'

'I know,' he said to the silhouette in the distance.

He'd checked for the SS blood-tattoos, he remembered that: the hot
stink there, inside of their left arms. But not the officer, the one with the
Iron Cross at his neck. He kept looking into the distance, up into the
burning sky. He smelled of French cologne. The edge was blunt by then,
or maybe his face was really tough. The skin kept being dragged by the
knife, not sliced, so he had to hold it flat, cursing, and work at it with a
sawing motion. Where was he? Oh yes. Here. By the end there was so
much blood his hands were getting slippery. He hated that: not being in
control. Hated it. He cut off the ears. The nose. The lips. He left the eyes,
so the German could see what had happened to him. So he would see.

★

*In the long light, soldiers still sleep under helmets and the loose summer earth
heaped up over them.*

★

The city closes down, finally. No sound, but the folding of knives.

★

222

'You have built temples,
multiplied fenced cities,' the boy in the blue suit
was speaking so quietly
he could hardly hear,
'But I will send a fire upon your cities,
and it shall devour your palaces.
The days of visitation are come.
You shall reap the whirlwind.'

★

He heard a short sharp bark, like a struck match,
saw the blank-eyed coyote loping away.

★

Under the orange sky, the mountains are on fire and you can see the
lines of flame moving up under the black smoke, the trees candle-
topping up the heights, burning the faces off the hills, hear the *pop,
pop, pop* of the propane tanks, the groan of houses falling into flames.
The chaparral's all burnt to ash, and rocks come loose and it all comes
landsliding down the sides of the mountains – sheds, cabins, cars,
decking, cottonwoods, sycamores, whole houses, propane tanks and
boulders the same size, pitching over the traps: the rumble of a bowling
alley, the clack of giant castanets, the shearing of metal like mortar-fire,
a train going off the tracks – the mountains sliding into Los Angeles.
Where the electricity poles were dancing where they stood, dogs running
backward and forward, cars rocking on their axles, birds panicking one
way, then the other, flying into walls, into each other; inside the buildings,
the furniture slithering, things shaken from their shelves, shelves tilting,
keeling, units rocking, shaking, toppling over, chairs rolling around on

their castors; pylons waggling, settling to a long singing, then rattling like jewelry till they snap, and start to whip and they're going down in lines, shorting out, like fire-crackers, severed snake-heads, the electric cables jerking, throwing sparks. Houses on the hills imploding, one by one. The aqueducts fracture, freeways buckle and snap; sand-fountains erupting in rows along the beach, the whole Los Angeles basin shaking like a bowl of jello. Palm trees are thrashing, every swimming pool in the city slopping wildly, parks now sudden lakes as the water-mains burst, broken sewer lines bubbling into the street, gas lines rupturing, the church bells going, ringing themselves. The buildings fail, block after block, the old downtown rows of brick-and-mortar just dissolve to dust, the new concrete ones cracking, collapsing, walls folding: glass shivered from its frames, cascading down in sheets. Only the wooden houses survive. Stands of trees go down like skittles. The fires jump the highways, embers sucked through the fire-tunnels of the canyons, feeding on the dry scrub and sagebrush, the gas lines throwing flame a hundred feet into the air. Tree-trunks stand as bent sticks in the fire-bed, the shells of cars slumped on burnt-up wheel-rims. The levelled ruins smoke. After-shocks shudder in waves, knocking out the last of the sirens. The ground opens, swallowing pieces of itself, cracking apart, rising in places to a twenty-foot cliff, and lifts now into two huge moving plates, under which something seems to be breathing.

*

If he could drain his eyes of this. The split world, the world
burning. The world, coming to grief.
The marriage of paper and fire. A living thing that crumbled
like a moth, into dust. Into ash. The making of ghosts.
He'd drowned it all. His youth,
the road's burning coal. The coal-seam fire inside.

But the slate is wiped clean ... *The slate is clean* ...
All sins are confessed, so the slate is *clean*.

★

Pike was following him, at a distance.
Click. Click. Click.

★

He saw old people dancing in slow-motion, in the scratchy
black-and-white of a ciné-film, moving in their long strathspey,
slow and stately to some silent fiddle and accordion, passing
through each other, through each other's hands and bodies,
the women turning
under the turning hands, disappearing. Ghosts of one another.
The film sticks; the projector judders to a halt, jams.
The celluloid burning yellow, bubbles; tearing to white.

click

He reached the corner of 5th and Pedro,
posting the knife with a *plip* through the ribs of a storm-drain,
laid down copies of the *Press* on the blackened sidewalk,
the one with the last of his bulletins,
then set his duffle bag on top.
Someone offered a cigarette, some pieces of bread,
another passed him a bottle, which he twisted open.
Thunderbird Red. It was the best thing he'd ever tasted.

click

He thought he could hear the weather: the last reel
played on the pipes, the wind in the trees, the sound of deer
running in the high fields.
He looked around at his comrades-in-arms, 'Remember me,'
then closed his eyes.
'I can stop now,' he said,
putting his mouth to the mouth of the bottle,
'I'll make my city here.'

CREDITS

PHOTOGRAPHS

Cover:

Hill Street Tunnel looking south from Temple Street on a fogbound night. The double tunnel connected Temple with 1st Street – Howard Maxwell, *Los Angeles Times*, 12 October 1954.

New York:

The Bowery under the shadows of the 3rd Avenue El, 1940s – Andreas Feininger (Getty Images).

Grand Central Station Sunbeams, 1940s – Underwood Archives.

Los Angeles:

Angels Flight and the 3rd Street Tunnel, looking west from Hill Street, with the 3rd Street steps on either side. The tunnel connected Hill Street and Hope Street – Los Angeles Public Library.

Selling papers on Olive Street – Loomis Dean, LIFE (Getty Images).

San Francisco:

Photograph of Coit Tower and Telegraph Hill, taken through the periscope of the U.S.S. *Catfish*, a diesel-powered US Navy submarine, passing under the Golden Gate Bridge in 1951.

Turk Street in the Tenderloin, 1950s (OpenSFHistory / wnp14.3613.jpg).

Los Angeles:

Looking east down 2nd Street, dead-ending at Olive Street and the parapet of the 2nd Street Tunnel, with the Mission Apartments on the immediate right – still from vintage footage (https://archive.org/details/ADriveThroughBunkerHillAndDowntownLosAngelesCa.1940s).

The Melrose Hotel, built in 1882 at Grand Avenue, between 1st and 2nd Street, demolished in 1957 – Los Angeles Public Library.

NOTES

p. vii – '*cos cheum nach gabh tilleadh*': Motto of the North Nova Scotia Highlanders – 'never a backward step'.

p. 12 – 'Watching *Ride the Pink Horse* . . .': *Ride the Pink Horse* (1947) Robert Montgomery (released 8 October, 1947).

p. 12 – '. . . then *Out of the Past*': *Out of the Past* (1947) Jacques Tourneur (released 13 November, 1947).

p. 16 – '*in some school round here*': St Paul's School, Hammersmith (south end of Brook Green; the school moved in 1968, and the buildings in Hammersmith were demolished in 1970), was the General Headquarters of the Home Forces. Montgomery, the Commander-in-Chief, was there from January 1944.

p. 26 – 'Margaree': Pronounced with a hard g, as in 'Margaret'.

p. 28 – 'Just finishing up here: Mott and Grand': The filming of *Cry of the City* (1948) Robert Siodmak: 26 December 1947 to 24 February 1948, New York.

p. 28 – 'you ever see *Brute Force?*': *Brute Force* (1947) Jules Dassin.

p. 43 – 'something good with Charles Laughton': *The Big Clock* (1948) John Farrow (released 9 April, 1948).

p. 43 – 'then *The Naked City*': *The Naked City* (1948) Jules Dassin (released 4 March, 1948).

p. 46 – 'San Pedro': Pronounced *Peedro*.

p. 69 – 'They were shooting in the 3rd Street Tunnel': The filming of *Act of Violence* (1948) Fred Zinnemann: 17 May to 15 July 1948, Los Angeles.

p. 70 – 'He goes down Court Street and sees cameras': The filming of *Criss Cross* (1949) Robert Siodmak: 14 June to 28 July 1948, Los Angeles.

p. 70 – '*goodbye to all we ever had*': Siodmak used the song 'I'll Remember April' repeatedly as a leitmotif for fated relationships in *Christmas Holiday, Phantom Lady, The Killers* and *Criss Cross*.

p. 71 – 'down in the storm-drains': The filming of *He Walked by Night* (1948) Alfred Werker and Anthony Mann (uncredited): 14 April to 31 July 1948. The storm-drain sequence may have inspired the Vienna sewer scenes in *The Third Man* (released 31 August 1949).

p. 71 – 'doing pieces in the *New York Sun*': For five months, beginning in October 1948, Siodmak and novelist Budd Schulberg worked together on a screenplay titled 'A Stone in the River Hudson', based on Malcolm Johnson's articles exposing corruption on the New York waterfront. The McCarthy hearings put an end to Schulberg's involvement and Daryl Zanuck sold the rights to Sam Spiegel, who produced the film with Elia Kazan directing, with the new title *On the Waterfront*. Siodmak sued in 1954 and was awarded $100,000.

p. 73 – 'the Hulbert, another SRO': SRO – single-room occupancy 'apartment hotels'.

p. 80 – 'snow on Angels Flight': From 9 to 12 January 1949, snow fell on Los Angeles.

p. 81 – 'all together as OLLYWOODLAND': The Hollywood sign is what remains of a 1923 advertisement for the 'Hollywoodland' real-estate development. In 1944, the sign was dilapidated (the 'H' having been destroyed in the early 1940s by a drunk driver, so it read OLLYWOODLAND), and the impecunious property developers transferred the deeds to the city, who agreed to repair it on the understanding that the 'LAND' would be dropped. The sign was rebuilt and restored in late 1949.

p. 84 – 'mopping out his cell': February 1949. Robert Mitchum was jailed for two months for possession of marijuana.

p. 90 – 'he went to see *Deadly Is the Female*': *Deadly Is the Female* (1950) Joseph H. Lewis (released on the west coast on 20 January under this title and on the east coast on 24 August renamed *Gun Crazy*). The two leads are John Dall and Peggy Cummins. The script was co-written by Dalton Trumbo, one of the then-blacklisted Hollywood Ten, who was imprisoned that year.

p. 94 – 'The new Widmark': *Night and the City* (1950) Jules Dassin (released 9 June 1950).

p. 97 – 'Three men in shirtsleeves': The filming of *M* (1951) Joseph Losey: 5 June to 7 July 1950, Los Angeles. Robert Siodmak's cousin, Seymour Nebenzal, had worked with Fritz Lang on the original *M* in 1931, and wanted to remake it. Given its subject matter – child-abduction and murder – Joseph Breen (Catholic censor, and administrator of the Motion Picture Production Code) said it could only be made if it followed the original script. Nebenzal hired various left-leaning actors and writers, and the former Communist Party member, Losey, to direct. Losey later said he took the film to make money in anticipation of blacklisting by the House Un-American Activities Committee (HUAC). Ernest Laszlo was director of photography and Robert Aldrich the assistant director.

p. 122 – 'O'Brien stayed there in *D.O.A.*': *D.O.A.* (1950) Rudolph Maté.

p. 122 – 'chased past its door in *The Lady from Shanghai*': *The Lady from Shanghai* (1948) Orson Welles.

p. 122 – 'Bacall's apartment in *Dark Passage*': *Dark Passage* (1947) Delmer Daves.

p. 126 – 'There's a film-crew outside': The filming of *The Sniper* (1952) Edward Dmytryk: 24 September to 20 October 1951, San Francisco.

p. 127 – 'On the cover of *Time* magazine': 22 October 1951.

p. 137 – 'past the Brocklebank': *The Lady from Shanghai*.

p. 137 – 'Agnes Moorehead . . . fire-escape': *Dark Passage*.

p. 138 – 'Joan Crawford leaves . . . 2nd Street Tunnel': *Sudden Fear* (1952) David Miller.

p. 149 – 'The CRA can do anything': The CRA (Community Redevelopment Agency) was created in California in 1948. Unaccountable and largely corrupt, the CRA was in thrall to the business community and the automobile industry. They demolished most of the old and historic residential buildings in downtown Los Angeles either to make way for freeways or for lucrative street-level parking, so dividing and reducing the local population and making street stores unviable as a result.

p. 155 – 'fountains in that Garden of Allah': The Garden of Allah was an exclusive and infamous hotel in Los Angeles, reputed to be the subject of the Joni Mitchell line: 'they paved paradise and put up a parking lot'.

p. 156 – 'Para todo mal . . . también!': 'For everything bad, mezcal! For everything good, the same!'

p. 161 – 'Back in March, he'd watched Ed Murrow': A special edition of Edward R. Murrow's 'See It Now' – 'A Report on Senator Joseph R. McCarthy' – was broadcast on CBS on 9 March 1954. It was the first open attack on McCarthy's witch-hunt.

p. 162 – 'the hearings started': From April to June 1954 the United
States Army was under investigation for Communist activities by
McCarthy's Senate Permanent Subcommittee on Investigations,
popularly known as the Army–McCarthy hearings. Joseph Welch
was the chief counsel for the army. McCarthy's legal adviser was
Roy Cohn, who had been instrumental in the 1951 trial of the
Rosenbergs for espionage and their subsequent conviction and
execution based on manipulated evidence. In the 1970s, Cohn was
the friend, mentor and legal adviser to Donald Trump.

p. 163 – 'there was a film-shoot going': The filming of *The Big Combo*
(1955) Joseph H. Lewis: 26 August to 21 September 1954, Los
Angeles.

p. 166 – 'Chaplin's old set-up': Charlie Chaplin Studios was built in
1917. Chaplin sold it in 1953, having left the US after a decade
of attacks from Hedda Hopper, HUAC and, finally, the attorney
general James Patrick McGranery, on charges of immoral conduct
and sympathy for Communism. It was known briefly as Kling
Studios, where *The Big Combo* was produced, and is currently the
Jim Henson Company Lot.

p. 166 – 'it was "Kike"': Joseph Lewis was born in New York, the son of
Russian Jewish immigrants.

p. 168 – 'He found a crew on Clay Street': The filming of *Kiss Me
Deadly* (1955) Robert Aldrich: 29 November to 23 December 1954,
Los Angeles. Ernest Laszlo was director of photography.

p. 175 – 'The Joe Lewis picture was opening': *The Big Combo* (1955)
Joseph H. Lewis (released on 13 February 1955).

p. 175 – 'how it got past the Code': Unaccountably, the Motion Picture Production Code passed a film that featured a pair of overtly homosexual hoodlums and a scene of oral sex.

p. 176 – 'Charlie Parker's died': 12 March 1955.

p. 178 – '*Kiss Me Deadly* was what it was called': *Kiss Me Deadly* (1955) Robert Aldrich (released on 18 May 1955).

p. 198 – 'I'm nobody's friend, the man with no place': *Ride the Pink Horse.*

p. 200 – 'her beautiful neighbor, the Melrose Hotel':The Melrose Hotel (a favourite of presidents Theodore Roosevelt and William McKinley) was demolished in 1957.The hotel was replaced with a temporary parking structure which is still standing today.

p. 208 – 'They'll pull down their house':The CRA didn't demolish Dr Green's old house at 232 S. Grand Avenue after his widow died, they moved in; it was their redevelopment office from 1963 to 1968.

p. 212 – 'Hey ... hey, I got this ... you know, I got this ticking noise ...': *Touch of Evil* (1958) Orson Welles (released 23 April 1958).

EPILOGUE

The Bunker Hill Urban Renewal Plan involved the eviction of 8–9,000 people, the removal of all structures on the 134 acres of Bunker Hill and the lowering of the elevation of the hill by up to 100 feet.The graded lots then became 'super-blocks' which were sold to developers at an estimated cost of $100 million. The clearances took place between 1959 and 1964, and involved the removal of 7,310 dwelling units and their occupants from 340 residential structures, and the demolition of 132 non-residential structures. The Sunshine Apartments building was destroyed in 1964.

ACKNOWLEDGEMENTS

With warm thanks to Robert Hass in Berkeley, Drenka Willen, Shelby White and the late Jean Stein in New York, Gary Kamiya in San Francisco, Ryan Gattis in Los Angeles and the MacLeods of Inverness County, Cape Breton; my gratitude also to Robert Stewart of Kansas City, Mona Simpson and Stephen Yenser at UCLA, and Alison Granucci.

My special thanks to Paul Baggaley and Emma Bravo, to Laura Morris and David Thomson, to Gary, again, for bar-work and picture-research, to Carole Newlands and Jack Niles for their generous hospitality in Berkeley and Boulder, and to Beatrice Monti Della Corte for her kindnesses over the years and for lending me her tower for a fifth time.

Among the many books I read, the most helpful was Howard Margolian's invaluable account of the execution of 187 Canadian prisoners-of-war in Normandy, *Conduct Unbecoming* (University of Toronto Press, 1998).

I'm indebted, as always, to my first reader, James Lasdun, to Don Paterson, my editor, and Peter Straus, my agent, and – particularly – Karin Altenberg, who has travelled with this book from the beginning.

bb

ぬ